THE LIVING WORD SERIES

edited by Gerard S. Sloyan

The Paschal Feast
in the Bible

by P. Grelot and J. Pierron

HELICON *Baltimore—Dublin*

Helicon Press, Inc.
1120 N. Calvert Street
Baltimore, Md. 21202

Helicon Limited
20 Upr. Fitzwilliam St.
Dublin 2, Ireland

Library of Congress Catalog Card Number 65-24131

Originally published in French under the title *La nuit et les fêtes de Pâques* by La Ligue Catholique de l'Évangile, Paris.

The text of the Confraternity Edition of the Holy Bible contained in this book is reproduced by license of Confraternity of Christian Doctrine, Washington, D.C., the owner of the copyright of said Holy Bible. Used with its permission. All rights reserved.

In citing passages from the Bible, the Confraternity of Christian Doctrine translation has been used whenever possible. "Yahweh" has been substituted for the English rendering, "the Lord," and proper names are spelled according to the usage of the Revised Standard Version. The numbering of the psalms corresponds to that of the RSV, with parenthetic reference to the CCD.

Nihil Obstat: Carroll E. Satterfield
Censor Librorum

Imprimatur: ✠ Lawrence Cardinal Shehan, D.D.
Archbishop of Baltimore,
December 15, 1965

The *Nihil Obstat* and *Imprimatur* are official declarations that a book or pamphlet is free of doctrinal or moral error. No implication is contained therein that those who have granted the *Nihil Obstat* and *Imprimatur* agree with the opinions expressed.

PRINTED IN THE UNITED STATES OF AMERICA

Contents

ABBREVIATIONS

Gen—Genesis
Ex—Exodus
Lev—Leviticus
Num—Numbers
Deut—Deuteronomy
Josh—Joshua
Judg—Judges
Ruth—Ruth
1 Sam—1 Samuel (1 Kings)
2 Sam—2 Samuel (2 Kings)
1 Kings—1 Kings (3 Kings)
2 Kings—2 Kings (4 Kings)
1 Chron—1 Chronicles
      (1 Paralipomenon)
2 Chron—2 Chronicles
      (2 Paralipomenon)
Ezra—Ezra (1 Esdras)
Neh—Nehemiah (2 Esdras)
Tob—Tobit (Tobias)
Judith—Judith
Esther—Esther
Job—Job
Ps—Psalms
Prov—Proverbs
Eccles—Ecclesiastes (Qoheleth)

Song—Song of Solomon
      (Canticle of Canticles)
Wis—Wisdom of Solomon
      (Wisdom)
Sir—Sirach (Ecclesiasticus)
Is—Isaiah
Jer—Jeremiah
Lam—Lamentations
Bar—Baruch
Ezek—Ezekiel
Dan—Daniel
Hos—Hosea (Osee)
Joel—Joel
Amos—Amos
Obad—Obadiah (Abdias)
Jon—Jonah
Mic—Micah (Micheas)
Nahum—Nahum
Hab—Habakkuk
Zeph—Zephaniah (Sophonias)
Hag—Haggai (Aggeus)
Zech—Zechariah (Zacharias)
Mal—Malachi (Malachias)
1 Mac—1 Maccabees
2 Mac—2 Maccabees

Mt—Matthew
Mk—Mark
Lk—Luke
Jn—John
Acts—Acts of the Apostles
Rom—Romans
1 Cor—1 Corinthians
2 Cor—2 Corinthians
Gal—Galatians
Eph—Ephesians
Phil—Philippians
Col—Colossians
1 Thess—1 Thessalonians
2 Thess—2 Thessalonians

1 Tim—1 Timothy
2 Tim—2 Timothy
Tit—Titus
Philem—Philemon
Heb—Hebrews
Jas—James
1 Pet—1 Peter
2 Pet—2 Peter
1 Jn—1 John
2 Jn—2 John
3 Jn—3 John
Jude—Jude
Apoc—Apocalypse

Chronology

PERSONS AND EVENTS	DATE B.C.	BOOKS OF THE BIBLE
Abraham	1900	
Isaac		Earliest oral tradition and written traditions which were later incorporated into Genesis
Jacob		
Joseph in Egypt	1500	
Israel in Egypt		
Moses and exodus from Egypt possibly under the reign of Ramses II of Egypt (1301–1234)	1250	Further developments of oral traditions. Laws and some associated traditions were put into writing
Joshua	1200	Records later used in the composition of the Book of Joshua
Judges		Records of contemporary heroes
Saul becomes king	c. 1030	
David becomes king at Jerusalem	c. 1000	Some psalms
Solomon succeeds David	970	Literary activity increases. State records collect material later used in Samuel, Kings and Chronicles
Solomon's temple begun	c. 965	Some wisdom literature

Event	B.C.	
The northern kingdom of Israel breaks with Judah	c. 930	The sacred history of the Yahwist, later used by the editors of the Pentateuch (i.e. the first five books of the Bible)
Elijah	850	The sacred history of the Elohist later used by the editors of the Pentateuch
Elisha	800	Amos; Hosea. Synthesis of Yahwist and Elohist narratives?
Samaria falls to the Assyrians: end of the northern kingdom	721	Isaiah (1–39 with some exceptions); Micah. During the reign of Hezekiah (716–687) considerable literary activity (Proverbs 25:1)
Jerusalem besieged by Assyrians	701	
	650	Zephaniah
Call of Jeremiah	627	
Discovery of the book of the law	622	
The fall of Assyria	612	Nahum. The great religious history of the deuteronomist school running from Joshua to 2 Kings
		Habakkuk (?)
Jerusalem captured for the first time by the Babylonians. First deportations	597	

PERSONS AND EVENTS	DATE B.C.	BOOKS OF THE BIBLE
Call of Ezekiel. Destruction of Jerusalem by Babylonians. Exile (or Babylonian captivity)	587	Jeremiah, Lamentations, Ezekiel, Isaiah 40-55
Fall of Babylon and end of the exile	539	
Some Jews return to Palestine	538	
Foundations of the second temple are laid	537	
	520	Haggai
	518	Zechariah
Ezra and Nehemiah active at Jerusalem	450	About this time the Pentateuch received its final form. The prophets Obadiah, Joel and Malachi were preaching. The following books were composed or received a more or less definitive form: Jonah, Job, Proverbs, Song of Solomon, Ruth, Ezra—Nehemiah and Chronicles, Tobit, some psalms and the final chapters of Isaiah (56-66)
Alexander captures Syria	333	
Greek translation of the Old Testament (known as the Septuagint)	300 c. 250	Ecclesiastes (Qoheleth), Baruch, Esther

	B.C.	
Maccabaean revolt	167	Daniel
	132	Greek translation of Sirach (Ecclesiasticus). 1 and 2 Maccabees. Judith.
	100	The book of Wisdom
Pompey takes Jerusalem	63	
Accession of Herod the Great	37	(The dates given for the books of the Bible do not prejudice the earlier or later dating of subsections of those books)
Birth of Jesus	6–7 (?)	
Death of Herod	4	
John the baptist begins to preach		
	A.D.	
Beginning of the public life of Jesus	c. 27	Earliest oral traditions
Death of Jesus—Easter. Coming of the Holy Spirit—Pentecost	30	Written sources later used by the authors of the four gospels
Martyrdom of Stephen and conversion of Paul	36–37	
Paul's first missionary journey	45–49	
Council of Jerusalem	49	
	50	Aramaic Matthew

9

PERSONS AND EVENTS	DATE A.D.	BOOKS OF THE BIBLE
Second missionary journey of Paul	50–52	1 and 2 Thessalonians
Third missionary journey of Paul	53–58	
	56	Philippians
	57	1 Corinthians, Galatians, 2 Corinthians, Romans, James
Paul a prisoner at Caesaraea	58–60	
Autumn: Paul's journey to Rome; shipwreck and winter in Malta	60	Colossians. Ephesians. Philemon
Paul freed. Journey to Spain (?)	63	1 Peter. Mark
Martyrdom of Peter	64 (or 67)	
	65	1 Timothy and Titus. Greek Matthew, Luke and the Acts of the Apostles (at latest, all before 80; others hold before 70). Hebrews; 2 Timothy
Martyrdom of Paul	67	
Jerusalem falls to the Romans; temple destroyed	70	Jude; 2 Peter
	c. 95	Apocalypse (Revelation). John and 1–3 John
Death of John	c. 100	

Introduction

THE PURPOSE OF THIS BOOK

Every year Christians are invited to watch during the
night of Easter. They spend the night recalling the occasions when God came to rescue his people. In doing so,
they accept an invitation which was given by God under
the old law, for the paschal vigil had long been an annual
practice when the new deliverance was accomplished by
Christ:

> This was a night of vigil for Yahweh, as he led them
> out of the land of Egypt; so on this same night all the
> Israelites must keep a vigil for Yahweh throughout
> their generations (Ex 12:42).

The feast of Easter is now above all the celebration of
the "passing" of Christ, and Christians "out of this world
to the Father" (Jn 13:1), "from death to life" (Jn 5:24;
1 Jn 3: 14), from the darkness of this world to the light
of eternal glory (*cf.* 1 Jn 1:5–6). Like the ancient Pasch,
however, it is still a multiple feast and includes the feast
of the Deliverance, the feast of the Unleavened Bread,
and the feast of the Paschal Lamb.

Many of us who are now privileged to attend the
Easter ceremonies think of them only in terms of Christ,

our paschal lamb, who delivers us by his sacrifice and is food for our souls. Yet to see only Christ and his contemporaries is to see but a part of the paschal scene. It is to overlook the background against which the leading figures stand out in the splendour of their true proportions. The scene is set for the celebration of the ancient Pasch and Christ appears to inaugurate the new. His actions and words are borrowed from the old; they are charged with the traditions of a thousand years, years which tell a nation's fitful service of a faithful God. On this sacred night, the nation begins a new era in its relations with God. To inaugurate it, Christ uses actions and words that are old; but Christ calls them new because they are different; the Church calls them eternal because they are perfect and final: "This is my blood of the *new* and *eternal* testament."

It is to help you to understand the setting in which Christ enacted our redemption that these pages are written, for in becoming the new Pasch, Christ came "not to destroy the law, but to fulfil it" (Mt 5:17).

WHAT BOOKS OF THE BIBLE MENTION THE PASCH?

The first traces of the paschal mystery are to be found in the second book of the Bible, the book of Exodus. There you will find the story of the exodus (going out) from Egypt (Chaps 3–15), to which frequent reference is subsequently made in the Bible. The liturgical laws governing the celebration of the Pasch in Israel are also recorded in this book of Exodus (Chaps 12–13), as well as in the remaining books of the Pentateuch (Leviticus 23; Numbers 9; Deuteronomy 16).

The book of Joshua shows that the march across the desert was closed by the celebration of the Pasch for the first time in the promised land (Josh 5:10–11). Then the historical books from Judges to Kings are strangely silent on this subject until the Pasch of Josiah in 622 B.C. (2 Kings 23:21–23). The Chronicler breaks this silence, however, when he mentions the Pasch of Hezekiah (726–697 B.C.) (2 Chron 30) and of Josiah (641–609 B.C.) (2 Chron 35). Continuing the history of Israel down to the restoration by Ezra and Nehemiah, he recalls the Pasch celebrated by the exiles on their return from captivity (Ezra 6:19–22).

There are few references to the paschal *night-watch* in the prophets (Is 30:27–33), although Ezekiel foresees its celebration in a passage where he speaks of the temple liturgy (Ezek 45:21–24). On the other hand, references to the paschal *deliverance* are numerous. When the prophets reprove the people for their unfaithful conduct, the gravity of their offence is measured against this act of Yahweh's generosity. The deliverance from Egypt is depicted as the pledge and the symbol of future acts of rescue on the part of Yahweh.

The same idea is found in the psalms. They sing of the great miracle of the past, as in Psalm 136(135), which is called the Great Hallel:

> Give thanks to Yahweh, for he is good,
>   for his mercy endures forever . . .
> Who smote the Egyptians in their first-born,
>   for his mercy endures forever;
> And brought out Israel from their midst,
>   for his mercy endures forever;
> With a mighty hand and an outstretched arm,
>   for his mercy endures forever (Ps 136(135):1, 10–12).

Some of the psalms (for example, 113(112)–118(117)) belonged to the paschal liturgy, and they must be read in that context if we are to grasp the meaning the Jews ultimately gave to them (*cf.* also Psalms 66(65); 77(76); 78(77); 105(104); 106(105); 114(113); 135(134)).

Finally the Wisdom of Solomon, when describing God's intervention to avenge the persecuted "saints," recalls his deliverance of the Israelites from the Egyptian persecution (*cf.* Wis 18–19).

From one end of the Old Testament to the other, the Pasch appears as a fundamental theme. History, prophecy, liturgy, meditation—all forms of literature make use of it. The night of deliverance lived on as a vivid memory in the minds of the Jewish people, and when Jesus accomplished the new deliverance, of which the ancient Pasch was the symbol and the promise, he did so on the occasion of the paschal feast. During the paschal supper he instituted the sacrament of the new Pasch, while reminding us that it is the symbol and promise of the eternal Pasch which will see us all united in the kingdom of his Father:

"I have greatly desired to eat this Passover [Pasch] with you, before I suffer; for I say to you that I will eat of it no more, until it has been fulfilled in the kingdom of God." And having taken a cup he gave thanks and said: "Take this and share it among you; for I say to you that I will not drink of the fruit of the vine, until the kingdom of God comes" (Lk 22:15–18).

The paschal themes of the Old Testament reappear in the books of the New, where they are applied to the feast of the Christian Pasch.

Since there is a certain growth in the understanding of the Pasch and some elaboration of its liturgy through the centuries, the texts of the Old Testament must be arranged in their chronological order, if this development is to be appreciated. The dating of Old Testament texts, however, presents peculiar difficulties because of the manner in which the various books came to be written. The historical books, for example, were often compiled from previously existing documents, which are then older than the book in which they appear. Sometimes too, the biblical writers drew on oral traditions as well as on written sources. The mere fact that these oral traditions had not been written down does not prejudice their historicity, and, of course, they may be many centuries older than the book in which they are ultimately incorporated.

These principles have been applied to the Pentateuch, or the first five books of the Bible, and while it is certain that these books ultimately derive from Moses, their contents have been edited and re-edited throughout their long history. The material which came from Moses was handed down, partly in writing and partly in oral tradition, probably in association with various sanctuaries in Palestine. On great festival days, the laws would be read and the ancient stories re-told to maintain the people's devotion to Yahweh, their Saviour. With the passage of time, these traditions reflected the interests and

1. Readers will more easily understand the arrangement of the texts in this booklet if they have read No. 1 in the series: *The Message of Moses.*

needs of the community with which they were associated. Diversity of interest brought variety in emphasis. Laws which in one place had lost their significance tended to be forgotten, while in another, they were retained and even amplified. The historical traditions were moulded in a variety of literary forms, which are often a tribute to the artistry of the writers and story-tellers through whom they passed.

More and more of these ancient oral traditions were put in writing, and with what was already written down, provided a wealth of material for anyone wishing to make a synthesis. Historical circumstance favoured such a synthesis, and at first two strands of tradition were brought together, with the addition later of a third and a fourth. Scholars claim to be able to distinguish these different strands in the close-spun thread of tradition, both written and oral, which the Pentateuch now presents, and has presented since before 400 B.C.

The four strands are generally designated the Yahwist, the Elohist, the deuteronomist and the priestly traditions. The Yahwist tradition was the first to take shape (? tenth century B.C.) and derives its name from the use of the proper name Yahweh for God, whereas the Elohist (ninth or eighth century B.C.) uses the common name Elohim (= God) instead. The distinction between the two traditions is not based entirely on this use of divine names. The literary character, the vocabulary, and the attitude to God are different in each case, and the traditions are associated with different parts of Palestine. The Yahwist tradition is at home in Judah, while the Elohist tradition developed among the northern tribes.

The deuteronomist tradition is incorporated in the

book of Deuteronomy; it seems to have been influenced by the teaching of the prophets, and especially by Hosea. While few traces of this tradition are found in the first four books of the Pentateuch, the presentation of the material found in the books of Joshua, Judges, Samuel and Kings is largely influenced by it. It is thought that this tradition was originally associated with the northern tribes, but it underwent a further development when it was brought to Jerusalem after the fall of Samaria in 722 B.C.

The priestly tradition developed among the priests in the temple at Jerusalem, and was largely concerned with genealogies, legal prescriptions and ritual, although narrative and didactic materials were not wanting. This tradition gave to the Pentateuch its definitive form during the post-exilic period (fifth century B.C.), and to it we owe the book of Leviticus as well as some short sections in Genesis, Exodus and Numbers. Its influence is to be found in the prophet Ezekiel, the books of Ezra and Nehemiah, and later in the books of Chronicles or Paralipomenon. The work of the priestly scribes, however, was not limited to the addition of new material; they also provided a chronological framework for the historical books of the Old Testament, including the Pentateuch, to which they prefixed their own account of creation (Gen 1–2:4).

This brief description of the growth of the Pentateuch taken in conjunction with the introductory remarks of each section will help the reader to understand the arrangement of the texts from the Old Testament, which we shall now consider in the following order:

(1) First come the Yahwist and Elohist traditions of

the Pentateuch. These embrace historical narratives and also some ritual and liturgical prescriptions which derive from them.

(2) The Deuteronomy tradition next merits our attention. It considers the same material from a different point of view.

(3) The place given by the prophets to memories of the paschal vigil and the paschal deliverance is then reviewed.

(4) The priestly tradition, reflected in the books of Ezekiel and Ezra, shows the paschal laws reaching a definitive form.

(5) Finally, the psalms, the work of the Chronicler, and the Wisdom of Solomon give some idea of the Pasch among the Jews of the last centuries before Christ.

Many precious customs and beliefs connected with this feast have not been recorded in the Bible, but are to be found in ancient Jewish writings, as, for example, in the legal tract *Pesachim* of the Mishna and Talmud, and in the book of Jubilees of the second century B.C. Brief mention of these shall be made.

The Pasch of Jesus and the Christian Pasch are thus set in the context which helped the apostles and first Christians to grasp their profound significance.

> Throughout all ages
> each one of us
> must regard himself
> as having come out of Egypt.
> —*Ritual of the Jewish Pasch*

PART I

The Pasch in the Old Testament

Prologue

Bible history describes God's frequent intervention to deliver Israel, often by an unexpected display of his power. For God is not merely "the creator of heaven and earth." He is the God of the old and the new Israel, and through his people Israel, his plans are being realised in history. In promise and fulfilment, he constantly brings relief to his people and, in each new crisis, the recollection of the deliverance from Egypt lends hope to their cries for help. It is *the* great act of rescue which bears the promise of a final deliverance far surpassing the deeds of old. The Israelites always look forward to the time when they shall live in the peace of God.

The Pasch first makes it appearance in the Old Testament in connection with the deliverance from Egypt and shares with it the place of honour in the memory of Israel.

The account of this great epic is found in Chapters 3 to 15 of Exodus, where it is interspersed with laws concerning the feast. In their present state, these chapters are a composition of different traditions, which all originate from Moses but vary in character and tone. When put together they make a rather complicated mosaic.

The pages which follow may help to discover its pattern.

CHAPTER ONE

The Early Traditions of Israel

As we have seen, many of the traditions of Israel were passed on orally in the first instance, but later crystallised in the most varied literary forms. The Yahwist account of the Exodus is probably to be attributed to the reign of Solomon (970–929 B.C.), which saw considerable literary activity in Jerusalem. The inspired writers who were responsible for this account worked on ancient materials—oral traditions which were already fixed and, especially in the case of laws, written documents. To the Yahwist account we owe much of the brightly written narrative of Exodus, Chapters 3–15, and the brief law code in Exodus 34, which is sometimes called "the ritual decalogue." From these texts one can learn how the Pasch was celebrated in Judah in the time of the first kings. Even then, however, the Israelites were following a traditional rite, whose origin was lost in the mists of antiquity.

The "ritual decalogue" of Exodus 34 depends on the group of laws contained in "the code of the covenant" (Ex 20:22 to 23:33), and there are excellent reasons for attributing this whole section as it stands, and not simply the material it contains, to Moses himself. He would have composed it when the Israelites settled in the plains of Moab after their departure from Egypt. Through Moses, then, we make direct contact with the period of the exodus itself.

The Elohist account of the departure from Egypt runs parallel to the Yahwist account, but is shorter and less complete. It took shape in the northern kingdom of Israel during the eighth century B.C. under the influence of prophetic teaching. The late date for this work of editing in no way prejudices the antiquity of the traditions recorded. In fact, one can notice a constant effort to preserve the authentic spirit of what was for the editors a golden age, the age of the exodus and wanderings in the desert.

Such are the sources which enlighten us concerning two main themes: the paschal lamb and the azymes (unleavened bread), two rites which were united in the annual commemoration of the exodus from Egypt.

THE PASCHAL LAMB

The immolation of the paschal lamb in Israel was a common form of sacrifice among Semitic peoples who led a pastoral life. At first, the lamb was sacrificed at the beginning of the year, as part of the first fruits, and the Bible shows its awareness of the antiquity of this practice by setting it in the dawn of human existence:

> Now Abel was a keeper of flocks and Cain a tiller of the soil. In the course of time Cain brought to Yahweh an offering of the fruit of the ground. Abel also brought some of his flock with their fat portions (Gen 4:2–4).

The first fruits belonged by right to God (Ex 22:29–30; 13: 11–16). To offer them to him was to invoke his blessing on the flocks and the harvest, and return thanks for the fertility bestowed.

1. *The sacrificial lamb.* The immolation of a victim,

however, had another meaning, a meaning which approaches more nearly to that of the Pasch. Even to-day certain nomads of the Near East, when they have slaughtered a lamb or a sheep, collect the blood in a vessel and sprinkle the pegs or the covering of their tents to protect them against evil spirits. Some semi-nomads sprinkle the lintels and door-posts of their fixed abode. Sacrifices of this kind are common when they come to live in a new tent or when an old one is enlarged. Such occasions often arise, when the semi-nomads change from their winter houses of stone to the tents in which they pass the summer.

In his book on the customs of Moabite Arabs, Père Jaussen quotes a sheikh as saying: "In the springtime, when I go again to live in my tent, I offer a sacrifice on the first evening. I do not offer just one sheep—that would be unworthy of me and my dwelling—but as many sheep as there are poles in my tent. I then sprinkle the poles and the entrance with blood." Even the Christian Arabs have preserved the custom of offering a victim and of sprinkling the lintels and door-posts of a new home. By this ritual, the non-Christians hope to placate the *jinn* (spirit) of the place, and to prevent reprisals for disturbing its peace.

These two ancient rites are found together in the Israelite Pasch: the sacrifice of the lamb in springtime, and the use of blood to protect oneself and one's home from all evil. It is therefore likely that these rites were practised in the time of the patriarchs and even earlier, when Israel was not yet a nation, and their fathers led flocks through the pastures of a land not theirs. With the exodus from Egypt, this ancient rite of the nomad shepherd acquires a vastly richer meaning; henceforth it is linked with the deliverance of Israel.

2. *"Let my people go to sacrifice in the desert."* In the story of the exodus from Egypt a detail of some importance is often overlooked. It is recorded by the Yahwist and recurs like a refrain in his account: it was on the occasion of the spring sacrifice that God delivered his people. Such is the implication of the order given by God to Moses:

> Then you and the elders of Israel shall go to the king of Egypt and say to him: Yahweh, the God of the Hebrews, has sent us word. Permit us, then, to go a three days' journey in the desert, that we may offer sacrifice to Yahweh, our God.
>
> Yet I know that the king of Egypt will not allow you to go unless he is forced. I will stretch out my hand, therefore, and smite Egypt by doing all kinds of wondrous deeds there. After that he will send you away (Ex 3:18–20).

Thus the great epic commences. It is a trial of strength between Yahweh, who has called his people to serve him, and Pharaoh, who refused to let them go. The plagues which scourge the Egyptians are God's weapons in this battle of giants. He is master of nature and disposes of its forces at will. The plagues foretold by Moses are the signs of his anger; they are the threats which Egypt is slow to understand because the Pharaoh's heart is hardened (Ex 7:3 etc.). Everything in the narrative contributes to the tension which grows from scene to scene, until Pharaoh, conquered at last, yields to a power greater than his own.

From the very first interview with the Pharaoh, Moses makes his mission clear:

The God of the Hebrews has sent us word. Let us go a three days' journey in the desert, that we may offer sacrifice to Yahweh, our God; otherwise he will punish us with pestilence or the sword (Ex 5:3).

There seems to be question of the ancient feast of the nomads, preceded by a three-day pilgrimage to the sacred place of sacrifice, perhaps the mountain where God appeared to Moses (Ex 3:1).

The proud king refuses permission to leave, and the plagues begin to ravage his country. At first he hardly heeds them (Ex 7:23), but soon pretends to yield:

Pray Yahweh to remove the frogs from me and my subjects, and I will let the people go to offer sacrifice to Yahweh (Ex 8:4).

When the plague ceases, Pharaoh recants and will not yield to the entreaties of Moses. Then comes the plague of flies:

Then Pharaoh summoned Moses and Aaron and said to them, "Go and offer sacrifice to your God in this land." But Moses replied, "It is not right to do so. . . . We must go a three days' journey in the desert to offer sacrifice to Yahweh, our God, as he commands us." "Well, then," said Pharaoh, "I will let you go to offer sacrifice to Yahweh, your God, in the desert, provided you do not go too far away and that you pray for me." Moses answered, "As soon as I leave your presence I will pray to Yahweh that the flies may depart tomorrow from Pharaoh and his servants and his subjects. Pharaoh, however, must not play false again by refusing to let the people go to offer sacrifice to Yahweh" (Ex 8:21–25).

Pharaoh again deceives the Hebrews. The Egyptian flocks are stricken down (Ex 9:1–3); still Pharaoh remains unmoved. The wrath of God falls on the crops; they are destroyed by hail. While Pharaoh feigns repentance, Moses is not impressed by his promises:

"I have sinned again! Yahweh is just; it is I and my subjects who are at fault. Pray to Yahweh, for we have had enough of God's thunder and hail. Then I will let you go; you need stay no longer." Moses replied, "As soon as I leave the city I will extend my hands to Yahweh; the thunder will cease, and there will be no more hail. Thus you shall learn that the earth is Yahweh's. But you and your servants, I know, do not yet fear Yahweh God" (Ex 9:27-30).

And so it happens. But Moses tries again:

Thus says Yahweh, the God of the Hebrews: How long will you refuse to submit to me? Let my people go to worship me. If you refuse to let my people go, I warn you, tomorrow I will bring locusts into your country (Ex 10:3-4).

Without awaiting an answer, Moses departs. The courtiers, in terror, intervene: "Let the men go," they said to their master. "Do you not yet realize that Egypt is being destroyed?"

Moses is recalled:

"You may go and worship Y hweh, your God. But how many of you will go?" "Young and old must go with us," Moses answered, "our sons and daughters as well as our flocks and herds must accompany us. That is what a feast of Yahweh means to us." "Yahweh help you," Pharaoh replied, "if I ever let your little ones go with you! Clearly, you have some evil in mind. No, No! Just you men can go and worship Yahweh. After all, that is what you want." With that they were driven from Pharaoh's presence (Ex 10:8-11).

But the locusts come, and Pharaoh's confidence is shaken:

I have sinned against Yahweh, your God, and against you. But now, do forgive me my sin once more, and pray Yahweh, your God, to take at least this deadly pest [lit., death] from me (Ex 10:16–17).

At Yahweh's word, the west wind sweeps the clouds of locusts into the Red Sea. Once again Pharaoh sends for Moses. What will his next move be?

"Go and worship Yahweh. Your little ones, too, may go with you. But your flocks and herds must remain." Moses replied, "You must also grant us sacrifices and holocausts to offer up to Yahweh, our God. Hence, our livestock also must go with us. Not an animal must be left behind. Some of them we must sacrifice to Yahweh, our God, but we ourselves shall not know which ones we must sacrifice to him until we arrive at the place itself." But Yahweh made Pharaoh obstinate, and he would not let them go. "Leave my presence," Pharaoh said to him, "and see to it that you do not appear before me again! The day you appear before me you shall die!" Moses replied, "Well said! I will never appear before you again" (Ex 10:24–29).

Moses then said, "Thus says Yahweh: At midnight I will go forth through Egypt. Every first-born in this land shall die, from the first-born of Pharaoh on the throne to the first-born of the slave-girl at the handmill, as well as all the first-born of the animals. Then there shall be loud wailing throughout the land of Egypt, such as has never been, nor will ever be again. . . . All these servants of yours shall then come down to me, and prostrate before me, they shall beg me, 'Leave us, you and all your followers!' Only then will I depart." With that he left Pharaoh's presence in hot anger (Ex 11:4–8).

The climax of the drama is reached. With each succeeding scene the tension grows, and the dénouement is anxiously awaited. All the plagues attributed to the

Yahwist tradition have been quoted: the bloody waters, the frogs, the flies, the cattle disease (murrain), the hail and the locusts—six in all succeed one another during a tragic week.[1] It is true that literary convention plays its part in the presentation of this story, but how otherwise could we grasp the religious drama underlying the events of history? The more obstinate Pharaoh shows himself, the more clearly does God give proof of his strength. In this struggle, God will have the last word, for he is the stronger.

We are here introduced to a most important theme of the Bible: History is like an enclosed battlefield on which the power of God, who wishes to put his merciful plan of salvation into effect, is in continual conflict with the power of darkness. From the beginning to the Apocalypse of St. John, the history of revelation records the activities of this mysterious opponent as he tries to thwart God's plan. He is often concealed behind the human agents he enlists to further his cause, but his efforts are in vain, for in the end victory belongs to God.

3. *The night of Yahweh's vigil.*

Moses called all the elders of Israel and said to them, "Go and procure lambs for your families, and slaughter them as Passover victims. Then take a bunch of hyssop,

1. In the final form of the narrative the list of plagues of the Yahwist account is mingled with material from two other sources, namely, the Elohist and priestly traditions. We shall return to the latter at a later stage (*cf.* p. 57). As for the Elohist account, it can be recognised by two distinguishing features: Moses works all his miracles by his rod (Ex 4:17–28; 7:9; 9:23a; 10:13a; 14:16; 17:5), and it is God himself who hardens the heart of Pharaoh (Ex 9:12; 10:20). The Elohist mentions four different plagues: the bloody waters, the hailstones, the locusts, and the darkness; finally, it describes the death of the first-born. When these traditions are combined, they give us ten plagues in all.

and dipping it in the blood that is in the basin, sprinkle the lintel and the two doorposts with this blood. But none of you shall go outdoors until morning. For Yahweh will go by, striking down the Egyptians. Seeing the blood on the lintel and the two doorposts, Yahweh will *pass over* that door and not let the destroyer come into your houses to strike you down. . . . Then the people bowed down in worship, and the Israelites went and did as Yahweh had commanded Moses and Aaron (Ex 12:21–23 and 28).

It is therefore in Egypt that the Pasch will be celebrated. It must have been well known to the people since Moses speaks of it as something which is taken for granted: "Slaughter them as Passover victims." Perhaps this was the feast of Yahweh they were to celebrate in the desert. In any case it incorporates two ancient Semitic customs:

a) the sacrifice of a small animal, whether sheep or goat, at the beginning of spring. The sequel will show there is question of "redeeming" the first-born of men by the sacrifice of the first-born animals;

b) the saving value of blood with which the doorposts of houses have been marked.

To understand the sequence of events, we must now recall an ancient principle of Semitic law, the so-called *lex-talionis:* "Eye for eye, tooth for tooth, life for life, wound for wound" (Ex 21:23–25). God will impose a similar penalty on Egypt, for he had said to Moses:

So you shall say to Pharaoh: Thus says Yahweh: Israel is my son, my first-born. Hence I tell you: Let my son go, that he may serve me. If you refuse to let him go, I warn you, I will kill your son, your first-born (Ex 4:22).

This threat explains the last calamity which befalls Egypt:

> At midnight Yahweh slew every first-born in the land of Egypt, from the first-born of Pharaoh on the throne to the first-born of the prisoner in the dungeon, as well as the first-born of the animals. Pharaoh arose in the night, he and all his servants and all the Egyptians; and there was a loud wailing throughout Egypt, for there was not a house without its dead. During the night Pharaoh summoned Moses and Aaron and said, "Leave my people at once, you and the Israelites with you! Go and worship Yahweh as you said. Take your flocks, too, and your herds, as you demanded, and begone; and you will be doing me a favour."
>
> The Egyptians likewise urged the people on, to hasten their departure from the land; they thought that otherwise they would all die (Ex 12:29–33).

The destroyer, the angel of death, has passed, busy in the execution of God's commands.

As we read these pages let us not forget that our story-tellers take greater interest in the supernatural causes of events, and in their deeper meaning, than in the natural means which God uses to produce them. In addition, Hebrew methods of composition lend themselves easily to the artificial grouping of facts, to the rearrangement of material, to summary accounts of events, which render more striking the supernatural aspect of the drama. The purely natural view of events will often escape our notice when they form a great religious epic, in which God himself is the hero. How better could one quicken the faith of readers who, century after century, will there find reasons for their faith in Yahweh, the God who has saved his people "with a strong hand and an outstretched arm" (Deut 5:15).

By its occurrence in the course of this deliverance, the Pasch acquires a new meaning. It is no longer just the sacrifice one offered to God in the spring; the blood of the lamb no longer serves just to protect the Israelite dwellings from evil. The Pasch has become a solemn reminder of the great deliverance, for Israel was saved by the blood of the lamb, when Yahweh dealt the Egyptians a mortal blow.

THE UNLEAVENED BREAD, OR THE AZYMES

In the account of the exodus from Egypt, which we have just quoted, there is a curious detail:

> The people, therefore, took their dough before it was leavened, in their kneading bowls wrapped in their cloaks on their shoulders. . . . Since the dough they had brought out of Egypt was not leavened, they baked it into unleavened loaves. They had been rushed out of Egypt and had no opportunity even to prepare food for the journey (Ex 12:34 and 39).

Certain historians think that the Azymes were originally a rite associated with agricultural communities. In the spring, when nature was being renewed, the feast of the first sheaf (Lev 23:10) came round. The new corn was milled, and new bread baked. For seven days, only unleavened bread was eaten. What was fermented, was regarded as ritually impure; one therefore abstained from such things when everything was being re-born. The old leaven was cast out, and man depended for nourishment on the new, unleavened, bread.

Others, however, see in the Azymes a detail which recalls the original nomadic state of the Israelite people. The nomadic Arabs of Moab use an unleavened bread, which is rapidly prepared and eaten hot, whereas in the villages salted bread, that has had time to ferment, is made.

Briefly, the origin of the Azymes is not at all clear. Even if there is question of an agricultural rite, it is not surprising to find it used by the Israelites in Egypt, since the descendants of the patriarchs, who were already semi-nomads in Canaan (Gen 26:12–14), devoted themselves to agriculture, as well as to raising cattle and sheep.

The most ancient sections of the Israelite laws mention the feast of the Azymes, for example, the code of the covenant:

> Three times a year you shall celebrate a pilgrim feast to me. You shall keep the feast of Unleavened Bread. As I have commanded you, you must eat unleavened bread for seven days at the prescribed time in the month of Abib [i.e., "of the ear of corn"=March-April], for it was then that you came out of Egypt. No one shall appear before me empty-handed. You shall also keep the feast of the grain harvest with the first of the crop that you have sown in the field; and finally, the feast at the fruit harvest at the end of the year, when you gather in the produce from the fields. Thrice a year shall all your men appear before Yahweh God (Ex 23:14–17).

These regulations which are reproduced with slight variations in the "ritual decalogue" (Ex 34:18, 22–23) govern a rite which was not confined to the family circle, for the eating of unleavened bread at home did not fulfil all obligations in regard to the festival. In addition, every man must go in pilgrimage to the sanctuary of Yahweh "to present himself before him" and make his offering. The first book of Samuel describes how Elkanah, the father of Samuel, faithfully conformed to this custom:

This man used to go up from his city annually to worship and sacrifice to Yahweh of hosts in Shiloh (1 Sam 1:3).

The text actually mentions only one pilgrimage as compared with the three prescribed in Exodus 34:23, but custom probably varied in this matter.

Since the Pasch and Azymes occurred at the beginning of spring, these two rites were united and acquired the same significance when Israel finally settled in the promised land. Together they recall the deliverance from Egypt:

> For seven days you shall eat unleavened bread, and the seventh day shall also be a festival to Yahweh. Only unleavened bread may be eaten during the seven days; no leaven and nothing leavened may be found in all your territory. On this day you shall explain to your son, "This is because of what Yahweh did for me when I came out of Egypt." It shall be as a sign of your hand and as a reminder on your forehead; thus the law of Yahweh will ever be on your lips, because with a strong hand Yahweh brought you out of Egypt (Ex 13:6–9).

We can now understand why the Azymes were introduced into the paschal meal itself:

> You shall not offer the blood of my sacrifice with leavened bread; nor shall the fat of *my feast* be kept overnight till the next day (Ex 23:18).

This prescription of the code of the covenant seems vague, but the ritual decalogue makes clear what feast is intended by implying that it was celebrated at night; it was a religious vigil:

> The sacrifice of the Passover feast [shall not] be kept overnight for the next day (Ex 34:25).

In each succeeding age the texts became more precise when sanctioning the customs firmly established in Israelite tradition. They manifest a reverence and care for what was Yahweh's feast *par excellence* (Ex 23:18 above). It recalled the great deliverance which was the divine sign on which every Israelite pinned his faith:

> When Israel saw . . . the great power that Yahweh had shown against the Egyptians, they feared Yahweh and believed in him and in his servant Moses (Ex 14:31).

THE ANNUAL COMMEMORATION

Israel therefore inherited ancient rites which already had a religious significance. The immolation of the first-born lamb and the observance of the week of Azymes recurred every spring, and were directed to the deity whose function it was to effect the rebirth of nature. In Israel, they acquired an entirely new meaning.

Israel went out of Egypt in the month of the ripening corn (Abib = March-April) when the Azymes were observed, and the celebration of the "feast of Yahweh" in the desert was the occasion of her departure. It was then that "the people of God" was born to history, and the Pasch was so closely related to these events that henceforth it became their memorial.

Israel will establish herself in Canaan, in the midst of a people given to the practice of fertility rites, but the Pasch will always have for her a totally different meaning. No longer is there merely question of honouring and petitioning the master of fruitful nature at the time of its restoration to life. The Pasch will evoke memories of the saving act of God by which he rescued his people and revealed something of his plan for the salvation of mankind. It will become the *anniversary of salvation* and thus reflect one of the characteristic aspects of the Christian Pasch.

Although we have used it many times, we have not yet explained the meaning of the word "pasch." Scholars are divided on the subject. Some have suggested that the name is derived from a verb meaning "to appease" (the divinity), but there is no proof that the Pasch was ever a sacrifice of appeasement, either in the biblical or pre-biblical periods. Others think that it may refer to a sacred dance which was originally performed during the feast (Ex 15:20; 32:19). In fact, the Hebrew verb describes some kind of dance performed around the altar by the prophets of Baal during the famous contest with Elijah (1 Kings 18:26).

The biblical texts give a popular interpretation of the name which recalls some of the events associated with the feast. On the basis of a possible meaning "to leap" for the Hebrew verb *pāsah*, from which Pasch is derived, they explain that during the dramatic vigil when Yahweh struck down the Egyptian first-born, "he leaped, or passed over" the Israelite homes which had been marked with the blood of the lamb (Ex 12:23; *cf.* 12:13). The Pasch is therefore the *passing* of the Lord when he mercifully spares mankind. The verb *pāsah* is found with the same meaning in Isaiah 31:5:

> Yahweh of hosts shall shield Jerusalem, to protect and deliver, to spare [*pass over*] and rescue it.

This may be an allusion to the deliverance of which we have just read an account.

CHAPTER TWO

The Book of Deuteronomy

Much of the Mosaic legislation found in the other books of the Pentateuch is presented in a revised form in the book of Deuteronomy, which reflects the needs of Israel under the kings.

The united kingdom of Israel and Judah had its greatest glory under David and Solomon. On the death of Solomon (931 B.C.) decay quickly set in, and the magnificent structure built by the energy and piety of these two kings quickly crumbled. The political breach involving the schism of the northern kingdom made it extremely difficult for the people of God to remain conscious of their spiritual unity. Moral and religious decline resulted in superficial worship of God by an elaborate ritual, which was meant to hide rather than to express the true sentiments of a people intent on breaking the law of God. The Israelites frequently ignored both moral and social laws, and gave themselves to the impure worship of Canaanite gods:

> This people ... honours me with their lips alone, though their hearts are far from me (Is 29:13).

If such was the picture in Judah where the tradition of David, the faithful king, still persisted, conditions in Israel were even worse, and it is there that the prophets first make their appearance: in the ninth century Elijah and Elisha, and about the middle of the eighth, Amos, a Judaean who preached in the north, and Hosea. Although mass conversions did not follow their preaching, some at least were fired by the prophets' ideal and became the faithful few in a forgetful people. Probably it is to this élite, many of them priests and scribes, that the book of Deuteronomy owes its origin.

What had these men in mind? Were they simply innovators? Far from it. They wished to bring Israel back to the law, to the authentic traditions of Moses. To achieve this aim, a revision of the law code became necessary; it must be adapted to the needs of the age. It was hoped that once again the voice of Moses would be heard, and would become a living force in a community which had forgotten its obligation to return the love of a loving God (Deut 6:4-9).

The fall of Samaria (722 B.C.) showed that this work was urgent. Shortly after this event which brought the northern kingdom to an end, some refugee priests may have deposited a revised copy of the Mosaic law in the temple at Jerusalem. This would have been the nucleus of our book of Deuteronomy (Deut 12-28). Another century was to pass, however, before the work received royal sanction under Josiah in 622 B.C. (2 Kings 22 and 23).

THE PASCH IN DEUTERONOMY

This brief sketch of the origin of the book shows that the spirit of the legislation in Deuteronomy is profoundly Mosaic. The influence of the Israelite prophets can also be felt in its pages which reflect a keen sense of social justice, and a powerful realisation of the rights of God.

One God, one people, one law, one national shrine, one form of worship—that was its program. The inspired law-makers looked beyond the period of the monarchy, which had brought disillusionment, to the time of the exodus, which was for them the golden age of Israel. Such was the practice of Hosea (Hos 2:16–17; 11:1–4); so would Jeremiah preach (Jer 2:2). All wished to re-live, at least in spirit, the ideals of the glorious past.

It is against this background that we must read the chapter devoted to the liturgical calendar (Deut 16). The ancient prescriptions of the earlier books re-appear in a modified form:

1. Observe the month of Abib by keeping the Passover of Yahweh, your God, since it was in the month of Abib that he brought you by night out of Egypt.

2. You shall offer the Passover sacrifice from your flock or your herd to Yahweh, your God, in the place which he chooses as the dwelling place of his name.

3. You shall not eat leavened bread with it. For seven days you shall eat with it only unleavened bread, the bread of affliction, that you may remember as long as you live the day of your departure from the land of Egypt; for in frightened haste you left the land of Egypt.

4. Nothing leavened may be found in all your territory for seven days, and none of the meat which you sacrificed on the evening of the first day shall be kept overnight for the next day.

5. You may not sacrifice the Passover in any of the communities which Yahweh, your God, gives you;

6. only at the place which he chooses as the dwelling place of his name, and in the evening at sunset, on the anniversary of your departure from Egypt, shall you sacrifice the Passover.

7. You shall cook and eat it at the place Yahweh, your God, chooses; then in the morning you may return to your tents.

8. For six days you shall eat unleavened bread, and on the seventh there shall be a solemn meeting in honour of Yahweh, your God; on that day you shall not do any sort of work (Deut 16:1–8).

Verses 1, 2, 5, 6, and 7 concern the paschal sacrifice, while verses 3, 4, and 8 refer to the Azymes. The law-makers have been so successful in fusing what were originally two separate rites, that the Azymes have simply become a part of the paschal feast.

The feast lasts seven days; it begins with a night of vigil, and ends with a solemn assembly. The date is fixed but not too precisely: in the month of Abib ("the ear of corn"). To the small beast prescribed when the Israelites were still shepherds is now added a large beast, which would come from the more highly developed farms.

This, however, is not the greatest change introduced by Deuteronomy. If we re-read the story of the Egyptian Pasch, which was based on ancient ritual, we notice it was a family feast. Now it has become a temple feast. It is no longer celebrated at home, for one must go to the temple of Yahweh during the paschal pilgrimage, which was originally attached to the feast of the Azymes. It is in the temple that the Pasch is immolated, and it is there that the sacred meal is eaten during the solemn vigil. On the following morning, the Israelites return to the booths (or tents) they had erected for their brief stay in the city, a custom imposed by practical necessity and by the memories it evoked of the time when they were nomads, the time when the Pasch became what it was: a memorial of the exodus from Egypt. Such practices were a perpetual reminder of the salvation wrought by Yahweh in Israel.

The scribes of the deuteronomist school return frequently to this last point. For them the Azymes were a bread of affliction (Deut 16:3) because they recalled a hasty departure into the night (Ex 12:32 and 39). These same scribes may have added some comments to the earlier legislation which now appear as part of the text of Exodus:

> Thus, you must also observe this rite when you have entered the land which Yahweh will give you as he promised. When your children ask you, "What does this rite of yours mean?" you shall reply, "This is the Passover sacrifice of Yahweh, who *passed over* the houses of the Israelites in Egypt; when he struck down the Egyptians, he spared our houses" (Ex 12:25-27).

This passage reminds one of the questions and answers of the baptismal ritual. When taking part in the ceremony for the first time, the young Israelite asks what it is all about. The answer is there, ready-made. It embraces the truths essential for Israelite faith; it explains what God has done for his people, how he has saved them in order to consecrate them to his service.

One other point in the deuteronomist legislation merits our attention. The law is expressed in the second person singular. Through the centuries it speaks to each Israelite as if he had personally experienced the great deliverance:

> In frightened haste you [singular] left the land of Egypt (Deut 16:3).

Everyone must, therefore, consider himself as personally involved in the mystery of salvation. The exodus is not simply ancient history which was commemorated annually: it is an act of God which touches most intimately each and every member of the people of God. The present day ritual of the Jewish Pasch expresses the idea in the following words:

> In every age, each one of us must look on himself as if he had come out of Egypt, as it is said: "You shall give this explanation to your son: It was with this purpose that the Eternal acted in my favor when I came out of Egypt." He did not deliver only our ancestors; he delivered us also with them . . . for many are the enemies who rise up to exterminate us. The Holy One (Blessed be his name) saves us from their hands. . . .

The same is true of the Christian Pasch. Jesus has accomplished *once for all* the mystery of salvation; but the grace of the cross and the resurrection touches each and every one of us personally. That is why the liturgy invites us each year to re-live in spirit the mystery of the Pasch. We are thus reminded that we really participate in the events we commemorate and are not idle spectators.

THE PASCH OF JOSIAH

The regulations of Deuteronomy were not immediately adopted in practice. They represented an ideal which was difficult to realise. So it happened that the book which was deposited in the temple remained forgotten and unread for many years. Eventually it was discovered by chance at the end of the seventh century, when repairs were being carried out in the temple at the order of King Josiah. When Hilkiah, the high-priest who was in charge of the work, found the book, he sent a message to the king saying:

> I have found a book of law in the house of Yahweh (2 Kings 22:8).

Josiah was a just man, a devoted servant of God, more than usually energetic and capable. It was he who undertook the reform of his kingdom on the basis of the laws of Deuteronomy.

That this reform was radical is clear to anyone who reads Chapters 22 and 23 of the second book of Kings; all idolatrous practices were suppressed, the pagan sanctuaries were burned and desecrated, and their ministers put to death; all the local sanctuaries of Yahweh, up to then regarded as lawful, were suppressed. The reformers had as their ideal: one God, one law, one temple! Those who drew up the laws of Deuteronomy did not perhaps foresee that this unification would benefit the royal sanctuary at Jerusalem. More probably they were thinking of the ancient tribal sanctuary, where the ark of the covenant was venerated (*cf.* Josh 8:30–35; 24:1–28, with Deut 11:26–32, and 27:4–26), but since David had brought the ark to Jerusalem (2 Sam 6), it had become the religious center of Israel; it was the place where Yahweh "made his name to dwell" (*cf.* Deut 16:6).

In short, Deuteronomy became state law. The centralisation foreseen for the celebration of the Pasch must be effected straight away. Once the covenant had been renewed (2 Kings 23:4–20), Josiah called to Jerusalem for a solemn feast (in 622) not only the people of Judah, but also the inhabitants of the old northern kingdom, part of which he had recently added to his territory:

> Thereupon the king commanded all the people, saying, "Keep the passover to Yahweh your God, as it is written in this book of the covenant." For such a passover as this had not been kept from the days of the judges who

judged Israel, and during all the days of the kings of Israel and the kings of Judah; but in the eighteenth year of king Josiah this passover was kept to Yahweh in Jerusalem (2 Kings 23:21-23).

By this we are not to understand that the paschal feast had disappeared from the religious life of Israel. It was simply a *family* feast when Josiah, in accordance with the law of Deuteronomy, made it a great *national* festival. By celebrating the anniversary of its birth to history, Israel became more conscious of her unity. The historians of Deuteronomy tell us it was so in the days of Moses, and during the first days in the land of Canaan. That was the golden age of the people of God; Josiah tried to restore it to Israel, that she might live in its spirit.

This was not easily accomplished. Opposition to the reforms of the king was considerable, and although it did not break into open rebellion, it hindered progress by a sulky and obstinate silence. The priests of Jerusalem viewed with displeasure a regulation which gave to priests of other sanctuaries the right to minister in the temple (*cf.* Deut 18:6-8 and 2 Kings 23:9), while the priests of the local shrines hardly approved of the decision to suppress these sanctuaries (Deut 12:13-14). In addition, the discontent of the superstitious masses had to be reckoned with, when they were forced to abandon Canaanite forms of pagan worship. Similarly, the law concerning the Pasch upset too many traditions to be accepted without question, for the practice of celebrating the Pasch at home was not only sanctioned by the ancient laws; it had long become a custom. As long as Josiah was alive, his orders were respected. No sooner was he dead than much of his work was nullified, and many of his reforms were questioned.

In 609, Josiah was killed in battle. He had pursued a

policy of national independence, both in regard to Assyria, whose power was on the wane, and to Egypt, his neighbour in the south. It was in defence of this independence that he met the Egyptian forces at Megiddo and lost both the battle and his life. The Pharaoh Neco nominated his successor (2 Kings 23:29–30), and under the last three kings of Judah (Jehoiakim, Jehoiachin, and Zedekiah), although Deuteronomy remained state law, in practice much of it was ignored. In these circumstances, the custom of celebrating the Pasch at home was probably revived. After the fall of Jerusalem (587) the élite of Judah were deported to Mesopotamia, or went into voluntary exile, and there is every reason to believe that they celebrated the Pasch in the land of their exile. It kept alive in their hearts the hope of a new deliverance based on a strong faith in Yahweh, the liberator of Israel.[1]

> It is not only one enemy
> who rises to exterminate us,
> but in every age
> someone seeks to wipe us out,
> and the Holy One, blessed be his Name,
> saves us from their hands.
>
> —*Ritual of the Jewish Pasch*

1. At present the Jews celebrate the Pasch every year, but the paschal meal no longer includes the paschal lamb, since it cannot be ritually slaughtered in the temple at Jerusalem. At the time of the first destruction of the temple in 587 B.C., Israelite law governing the place for celebrating the paschal feast was still in a fluid state. It is therefore probable that the paschal meal was eaten during the exile, at least by those who adhered to the more ancient practice of eating the paschal meal at home. This diversity of practice may have continued up to the time when the law governing the feast was finally codified (*cf.* below p. 68). Many historians, however, take the view that after 622 B.C. the paschal meal was never eaten outside Jerusalem except by a few splinter groups. Even in this view one may suppose that an annual feast was celebrated with an incomplete ritual, as is done to-day.

CHAPTER THREE

The Prophets and the New Exodus

THE PASCH IN THE PROPHETS

The recollection of the great deliverance of old is continually present to the memory of the prophets; for them it was the great manifestation of Yahweh's love for Israel:

> When Israel was a child I loved him,
>   out of Egypt I called my son (Hos 11:1).

> By a prophet Yahweh brought Israel out of Egypt,
>   and by a prophet they were protected (Hos 12:14).

> I am Yahweh, your God, since the land of Egypt;
>   I will again have you live in tents,
> as in that appointed time (Hos 12:10).

These texts re-echo the answer to be given to the enquiring son during the paschal vigil, but references to the vigil itself are extremely rare in the prophets. This is also true of the other feasts. Hosea speaks of "the days of assembly," "the day of the feast of Yahweh," but he most probably refers to the autumn festival, elsewhere described as "the feast of tabernacles [or tents]." Isaiah is more explicit. Already in 9:2, in describing the messianic deliverance, he compares the joy of *that day* to the noisy jubilation of the harvest festival, whereas in Chapter 30:29, he uses the joy of the paschal vigil as his term of comparison.

The prophecy was uttered during the period of Assyrian supremacy, probably at the time when the armies of Sennacherib had laid siege to Jerusalem (701 B.C.). The inhabitants were paralysed with fear, but Isaiah lived in hope. He foretold with calm certainty the chastisement and ruin of Assyria, which in its pride had raised itself against God (*cf.* Is 37:21–35; 10:5–19; 31:4–9). Against such a background, he paints this picture of the future deliverance:

> See the name of Yahweh coming from afar
> in burning wrath, with lowering clouds!
> His lips are filled with fury,
> his tongue is like a consuming fire;
> His breath, like a flood in a ravine
> that reaches suddenly to the neck. . . .
>
> You will sing
> as on a night when a feast is observed,
> And be merry of heart,
> as one marching along with a flute
> Toward the mountain of Yahweh,
> toward the Rock of Israel (Is 30:29).

The prospect of a new deliverance creates an atmosphere of paschal joy amongst the Israelites, and they love to recall the exodus from Egypt, as they fête the God who will deliver them by yet another miracle. Though the present is bitter and hard to bear, it presents a challenge to Yahweh to renew the wonders of the exodus, that the designs of his love may find their fulfilment in his people.

THE EXPECTATION OF THE NEW EXODUS

The same hope rings through the messianic promises, and its tones resound more clearly as the trials of Israel increase and its burdens become harder to bear. We may recall the terms in which the prophets depict the "last times" (*cf.* Is 2:2; Acts 2:17, etc.), those days when God will fulfil for his people, now chastened and converted, the promises of Sinai, whose realisation was so often obstructed by their sins. They describe the future in terms of an idealised past. A fresh start will be made: a new deliverance, a new exodus, a new covenant, a new law, a new crossing of the desert, a new entry into a promised land, identified with paradise regained; a new king, greater than David and Solomon; a new temple, more magnificent than the old, in a new Jerusalem, where God will dwell for ever. . . . The splendour of the future will obscure the very memory of the past:

> Therefore, the days will come, says Yahweh, when they shall no longer say, "As Yahweh lives, who brought the Israelites out of the land of Egypt"; but rather, "As Yahweh lives, who brought the descendants of the house of Israel up from the land of the north"—and from all the lands to which I banished them; they shall again live on their own land (Jer 23:7–8).

The exiled Jews dream of the salvation of other days; it is the measure and the sign of the salvation they now await:

> Then they remembered the days of old
> and Moses, his servant;
> Where is he who brought up out of the sea
> the shepherd of his flock?
> Where is he who put his holy spirit
> in their midst;
> Whose glorious arm
> was the guide at Moses' right;
> Who divided the waters before them,
> winning for himself eternal renown;
> Who led them without stumbling through the depths. . . .

Look down from heaven and regard us
from your holy and glorious palace!
Where is your zealous care and your might,
your surge of pity and your mercy?
O Yahweh, hold not back
for you are our father.
Were Abraham not to know us,
nor Israel to acknowledge us,
You, Yahweh, are our father,
our redeemer you are named forever.

Oh, that you would rend the heavens and come down,
with the mountains quaking before you. . . .
Thus your name would be made known to your enemies
and the nations would tremble before you,
While you wrought awesome deeds we could not hope for
        (Is 63:11–13a; 63:15–16; 63:19b and 64:1b and 2).

The same theme recurs with variations in the *book of consolation*. This title is given to a collection of prophecies which were composed towards the end of the Babylonian captivity (587–538 B.C.) by an unknown, but inspired, writer. He may have belonged to a group which ultimately owed its origin to the disciples of Isaiah, for his writings often reflect the thoughts of the great prophet, and have been preserved as Chapters 40–55 of the book of Isaiah:

Comfort, give comfort to my people,
says your God.
Speak tenderly to Jerusalem, and proclaim to her
that her service is at an end,
her guilt is expiated;
Indeed, she has received from the hand of Yahweh
double for all her sins.

A voice cries out:
In the desert prepare the way of Yahweh!

Make straight in the wasteland a highway for our God!
Every valley shall be filled in,
every mountain and hill shall be made low;
the rugged land shall be made a plain,
the rough country, a broad valley.
Then the glory of Yahweh shall be revealed,
and all mankind shall see it together;
for the mouth of Yahweh has spoken.

A voice says, "Cry out!"
I answer, "What shall I cry out?"
"All mankind is grass,
and all their glory like the flower of the field.
The grass withers, the flower wilts,
when the breath of Yahweh blows upon it.
(So then, the people is the grass.)
Though the grass withers and the flower wilts,
the word of our God stands forever."

Go up onto a high mountain,
Zion, herald of glad tidings;
Cry out at the top of your voice,
Jerusalem, herald of good news!
Fear not to cry out
and say to the cities of Judah:
Here is your God!
Here comes with power
Yahweh God,
who rules by his strong arm;
Here is his reward with him,
his recompense before him.
Like a shepherd he feeds his flock;
in his arms he gathers the lambs,
Carrying them in his bosom,
and leading the ewes with care (Is 40:1–11).

How striking is this return of the liberated people! In
the desert is laid a triumphal highway along which goes
Yahweh at the head of his people—just as in the days of

old, when he led them in the pillar of cloud. He is the shepherd, and Israel is his flock. His sheep can walk without fear, for he is their guide:

> But now, thus says Yahweh,
> who created you, O Jacob, and formed you, O Israel:
> Fear not, for I have redeemed you;
> I have called you by name; you are mine.
> When you pass through the water, I will be with you;
> in the rivers you shall not drown.
> When you walk through fire, you shall not be burned;
> the flames shall not consume you.
> For I am Yahweh, your God,
> the Holy One of Israel, your saviour (Is 43:1–3a).

> Thus says Yahweh,
> who opens a way in the sea
> and a path in the mighty waters,
> Who leads out chariots and horsemen,
> a powerful army,
> Till they lie prostrate together, never to rise,
> snuffed out and quenched like a wick.
> Remember not the events of the past,
> the things of long ago consider not;
> See, I am doing something new!
> Now it springs forth, do you not perceive it?
> In the desert I make a way,
> in the wasteland, rivers.
> Wild beasts honor me,
> jackals and ostriches,
> For I put water in the desert
> and rivers in the wasteland
> for my chosen people to drink,
> The people whom I formed for myself,
> that they might announce my praise (Is 43:16–21).

The allusions in these texts would lead us to suppose that they are closely related to the celebration of the

Pasch. They are, in a sense, commentaries on ancient traditions, such as the Jews would later know in the synagogues, where the Scriptures were read and commented on in the course of the liturgical year. The exiled Jews looked for consolation in the reading of those sacred books which were already in existence, and they celebrated their ancient ritual in a foreign land, in so far as the absence of the temple permitted.

The Jewish institution known as the synagogue takes its origin from this period in Israel's history. The word itself means "a collection" and when used of men assembled for a religious purpose could be translated by "congregation." During the exile the Jews used to meet to pray, and since the absence of the temple rendered sacrifice impossible the services consisted in readings from the law, singing of psalms, and explanation of the prophetical writings. Even though it is probable that some groups used to eat the paschal meal in exile, this is hardly likely in those circles from which the "book of consolation" (Is 40–55) derived, as it is strongly influenced by Deuteronomy which insisted that the paschal lamb be slaughtered in the temple. There is no doubt, however, that even where the lamb was not eaten, the Jews used to read the parts of Scripture associated with the feast. Every year, springtime reminded them of the exodus, a memory which was sad in the context of captivity, but encouraging in the hope it inspired. In the distant past, God had revealed his plan of salvation and the might of his arm. Yahweh would intervene yet again; of this, the annual celebration of the ancient Pasch was the guarantee. When the Jews ate the paschal lamb, they did not think of the past alone, but looked forward to the "new thing" (Is 43:19) promised for the future, to the Pasch of the messianic times.

> Remember not the events of the past,
> the things of long ago consider not;
> see, I am doing something new!

CHAPTER FOUR

The Priestly Legislation

The exile was a period of reflection and prayer during which the Jewish élite, the "remnant" of Isaiah (Is 10: 20–21), was converted, and following the precepts of Deuteronomy, they set about impressing the law of God on their hearts (Deut 6:6; cf. Jer 31:33, and Is 51:7). It was, too, a time of study and work, when the Jews applied themselves to the task of collecting and preserving the legacy of the past laws, ritual, psalms, prophecies, and proverbs. As a preparation for the future, it was essential to formulate the law of Israel with the utmost precision since Deuteronomy and the older collection of laws were already regarded by the Babylonian conqueror—and later by the Persian king—as the official law of the land of Judah, as we can see in the books of Ezra and Nehemiah. The religious customs, written and unwritten, constituted a rich inheritance, which must not be lost in the period of crisis which had scattered the nation to the corners of the earth.

During the exile, therefore, the more fervent of the Judaean priestly caste formed groups for the study of law and the deepening of the spiritual life. Such groups are associated especially with the prophet Ezekiel, and are generally identified with those schools of scribes which were founded in Babylon, and remained active for several centuries. Ezra is one of the best known graduates of these schools.

In the book of the prophecies of Ezekiel, the appeals for repentance, the oracles against the pagan nations, and the eschatological promises are followed by some plans for the future. They are rather curious plans for they combine the most idealistic projects, impossible to realise in practice (Ezek 47:21 to 48:29), with some very precise and concrete instructions. Chapters 40 to 48 of the book of Ezekiel deal with these plans, and since the general tone of the section is legal, it is often called the torah, that is, the law, of Ezekiel. It is there that we find the liturgical calendar:

> On the first day of the first month you shall use an unblemished young bull as a sacrifice to purify the sanctuary. Then the priest shall take some of the blood from the sin offering and put it on the doorposts of the temple, on the four corners of the ledge of the altar, and on the doorposts of the gates of the inner court. You shall repeat this on the first day of the seventh month for those who have sinned through inadvertence or ignorance; thus you shall make atonement for the temple. On the fourteenth day of the first month you shall observe the feast of the Passover; for seven days unleavened bread is to be eaten. On that day the prince shall offer on his own behalf, and on behalf of all the people of the land, a bull as a sin offering. On each of the seven days of the feast he shall offer as a holocaust to Yahweh seven bulls and seven rams without blemish, and as a sin offering he shall offer one male goat each day. . . . On the fifteenth day of the seventh month, the feast day [i.e., of Tabernacles], and for seven days,

he shall perform the same rites, making the same sin offerings (Ezek 45:18-25).

A striking feature of these texts is the rather sudden importance given to the expiation of sins. This epoch-making result of the captivity was the fruit of a prolonged and prayerful examination of the national conscience. Continual contemplation of their infidelity awoke in the Jews a desire of ever more effective purification (*cf.* Ezek 36:16-37).

The rites of expiation which Ezekiel incorporated in his projected legislation, in all probability formed part of the ritual in the pre-exilic temple at Jerusalem. What was new was the introduction of this idea of expiation into the feasts of the Pasch and Tabernacles, which until then served a different purpose. The annual day of expiation (Lev 16; 23:26-32; Num 29:7-11), which was devoted exclusively to this purpose, no longer sufficed for the expiation of sin, and preoccupation with sin now dominates the ritual of all feasts, and puts a brake on the joy of the paschal vigil.

Ezekiel is also the first witness to the fixing of an important date in the calendar; the Pasch is to be celebrated on the fourteenth day of the first month, in the evening, and is to be followed by seven days of Azymes. This is not exactly what is prescribed in Deuteronomy (*cf.* above p. 40), and, in addition, Ezekiel's calendar follows the Babylonian system of reckoning, which is used in most of the works which come from the priestly tradition.

When was this calendar introduced into Israel? One can only conjecture. It was most probably in use in the temple before the captivity; Ezekiel would then preserve the earlier practice. The beginning of the first month was determined by the new spring moon, so that the paschal vigil in the priestly calendar would coincide with the full moon.[1]

We may sometimes wonder why the date of our Pasch (Easter) changes so capriciously from year to year. The explanation is to be found in the practice of fixing our Easter according to the reckoning of the lunar year, in which Easter Sunday is the Sunday immediately following the full spring moon. In this respect, our liturgical calendar follows its ancient model.

BIBLE HISTORY ACCORDING TO THE PRIESTLY TRADITION

It is exceedingly difficult to follow every detail of the work of compilation and codification carried out by the priestly schools during the exile, and when, following the decree of Cyrus (538), worship in Jerusalem was revived and the temple reconstructed (515), we can only wonder to what extent the temple practice coincided with the legislation which had been hammered out in exile. Was Deuteronomy, which had been the state law of Judah before the exile, now effectively put in practice? We cannot say with certainty.

1. It is not easy to say whether the ancient Israelite calendar began in the autumn, or in the spring like the priestly calendar mentioned above. The latter calendar may not always have been understood as the Pharisees understood it in the time of Christ. They reckoned twelve lunar months to the year with the insertion of an intercalary month when necessary, but the Essenes at Qumran, who were contemporary with Christ, had a calendar of 364 days which began on the first of Nisan (March-April). In this calendar, the Pasch always fell on the same date and day—a Tuesday evening. The priestly tradition of the Old Testament writings may have been following this usage, which could then be regarded as the earliest interpretation of the regulations governing the date of the Pasch.

At all events, the priestly legislators decided at a certain stage to set their legal reforms in a vast framework of biblical history. In much the same way, the ancient Yahwist and Elohist traditions had already provided the setting for the earlier laws of which we have spoken. This Bible history according to the priestly tradition sketched in broad outline the unfolding of God's plan, while marking clearly its important stages: the creation (Gen 1), the flood and the first covenant with Noah (Gen 6–9), the call of Abraham and the second covenant sealed by the sign of circumcision (Gen 12:4b–5; 17), the exodus and the third covenant which gave to Israel most of its civil and liturgical laws.

Naturally, this last stage was the most highly developed. It included an account of the call of Moses (Ex 6:2–13), and of the exodus from Egypt. Four plagues succeeded one another uninterruptedly: the bloody waters (Ex 7:19–20a, 21b–22), the frogs (Ex 8:1–3,11b), the mosquitoes (Ex 8:16–20), the boils (Ex 9:8–12). Thus the narrative worked towards the dénouement, for "Yahweh had hardened the heart of Pharaoh and he would not let the Israelites leave his land" (Ex 11:10). Just as had happened in the Yahwist traditions, the ritual of the Pasch was interwoven with the thread of history. It is the same ancient ritual that we have already seen, but now more detailed and adapted to suit the character of the priestly legislation:

Yahweh said to Moses and Aaron in the land of Egypt, This month shall stand at the head of your calendar; you shall reckon it the first month of the year. Tell the whole community of Israel: On the tenth of this month every one of your families must procure for itself a lamb, one apiece for each household. If a family is too small for a whole lamb, it shall join the nearest household in procuring one and shall share in the lamb in proportion to the number of persons who partake of it.

The lamb must be a year old male and without blemish. You may take it from either the sheep or the goats. You shall keep it until the fourteenth day of this month, and then, with the whole assembly of Israel present, it shall be slaughtered during the evening twilight [lit., between the two evenings]. They shall take some of its blood and apply it to the two doorposts and the lintel of every house in which they partake of the lamb. That same night they shall eat its roasted flesh with unleavened bread and bitter herbs. It shall not be eaten raw or boiled, but roasted whole, with its head and shanks and inner organs. None of it must be kept beyond the next morning; whatever is left over in the morning shall be burned up.

This is how you are to eat it: with your loins girt, sandals on your feet and your staff in hand, you shall eat like those who are in flight. It is the Passover of Yahweh. For on this same night I will go through Egypt, striking down every first-born of the land, both man and beast, and executing judgment on all the gods of Egypt—I, Yahweh! But the blood will mark the houses where you are. Seeing the blood, I will *pass over* you; thus, when I strike the land of Egypt, no destructive blow will come upon you.

This day shall be a memorial feast for you, which all your generations shall celebrate with pilgrimage to Yahweh as a perpetual institution (Ex 12:1–14).

This historical synthesis of the priestly school is dominated by the idea that Israel is not like any other people or race. They are a "community," "a sacred assembly," brought together by Yahweh for his greater glory and set apart for his service. One might even refer to them as his Church, for the word *ekklesia* was used by the Greek translators of the Old Testament to convey precisely this idea. It is after this model that the group leaving Egypt is portrayed. But as yet there is no temple, and the Pasch remains a family feast, a feast of nomads and of shepherds, as is indicated by the dress of the participants. The ancient rites are duly respected and preserved, but the celebration of this feast is not reserved to the central shrine, as was the case in Deuteronomy, for who would ever think of preventing its celebration in exile? The priestly legislators had too much respect for ancient custom to think of changing the law on this point.[2]

Although derived from ancient tradition, the ritual calendar of the priests is the same as Ezekiel's. Apparently both the priests and Ezekiel made use of the document now inserted in Chapter 23 of Leviticus, in the section known as "the code of holiness" (Lev 17–26)[3]:

These, then, are the festivals of Yahweh which you shall celebrate at their proper time with a sacred assembly. The Passover of Yahweh falls on the fourteenth day of the first month, at the evening twilight. The fifteenth day of this month is Yahweh's feast of Unleavened

2. Even before they had described the construction of the tabernacle in the desert, the historical writers of the priestly group introduced into their narrative such essential laws as could be observed anywhere, e.g., the laws governing the sabbath, food and circumcision. This is also true of the Pasch.

3. The code of holiness is a clearly defined unit within the body of the priestly writings. It gets its name because of its insistence on holiness: "Be ye holy, for I am holy" (Lev 19:2). This code was probably composed before the exile since Ezekiel seems to depend on it. It was subsequently altered as is clear from Leviticus 23 where the ancient calendar of the code of holiness is combined with the priestly reckoning.

Bread. For seven days you shall eat unleavened bread. On the first of these days you shall hold a sacred assembly and do no sort of work. On each of the seven days you shall offer an oblation to Yahweh. Then on the seventh day you shall again hold a sacred assembly and do no sort of work (Lev 23:4–8).

Although the two feasts of the Pasch and the Azymes are here less closely linked than in Deuteronomy, the text insists on the complete dedication of a week to the feast, which begins and ends with days of rest, analogous to the sabbath day repose.

Once the Pasch had been instituted, its re-appearance in the priestly history of Israel is not surprising. On the anniversary day of the exodus from Egypt, the Israelites celebrate it in the wilderness of Sinai (Num 9:1–5). When the Jordan was eventually crossed, the Israelites camped at Gilgal and there celebrated the first Pasch in the promised land, at which the azymes were made from the first fruits of the country they had just entered (Josh 5:10–12).

In selecting the events for record, the historians are motivated by the thought of Israel in the desert, which is for them the ideal concept of the people of God. Israel will live through a turbulent history, and although dispersed amongst the nations, she will preserve her national and religious identity. No matter where her captors lead her, the paschal feast is a source of inspiration, and the entry into the promised land a symbol of the "rest of God" (Ps 95(94):11; Heb 3:11,18) which awaits her in the messianic times, and to which she looks forward in the dark days of suffering and exile (cf. Ezek 36:24–38). The Pasch of the Israelites under Joshua, celebrated when they first entered the promised land, is no empty recollection of history. It is a promise of the new Pasch to be celebrated when the day of salvation shall dawn. . . .

THE PASCH AT ELEPHANTINE

The obscurity of the early post-exilic period (538 B.C. onwards) hides many of the sorrows which met those who returned to their ruined city. Little progress in rehabilitation was made until Nehemiah arrived (c. 445 B.C.). With the support of the Persian authorities, he rebuilt the walls of Jerusalem and re-organised the administration of the province of Judah, which was now withdrawn from the control of Samaria and became autonomous within the vast empire of the Persian kings (Neh 1–12). He also undertook the internal reform of Judaism on the basis of the laws which were already in existence. Although vigorously opposed by the Samaritan aristocracy, he repelled all their attacks, and showed himself completely independent in refusing to ratify the mixed marriage of the high-priest's son with a Samaritan (Neh 13:28).

Nehemiah's two successful missions re-established Judah as the religious center of the Jewish people who were now scattered abroad from upper Egypt to the cities of Persia and Media. Trade may have brought some even as far as India, Southern Arabia and Libya. On the island of Elephantine in the Nile, just opposite Assuan, a Jewish military colony had been established, long before the conquest of Egypt by Cambyses in 525 B.C., to guard the frontier and protect the royal highways. The religion of these exiled Jews is a curious mixture of orthodoxy and paganism, and may reflect the condition of Judah before the reforms of Josiah (639–609). They know nothing of the law of Deuteronomy, or, at least, ignore it, because they have a temple of their own in which Yahweh is honoured amongst other gods. They have preserved many of the ancient rites they brought from their native land, perhaps two hundred years earlier, and they celebrate the Pasch. A fifth century letter written on a piece of sherd by one of the group, bore the laconic question: *When will you celebrate the Pasch?* Apparently the liturgical calendar was not too precise on the point, no more than it had been in the older period, when one celebrated the Pasch in the "month of the ear [of corn]."

In the year 419, the Jews of Elephantine received a rather curious letter. Its writer, Hananiah, is an official representative of the Persian administration, which for some reason is concerned with the celebration of the Pasch and the Azymes there:

> To my brethren, Yedoniah and his colleagues, the Jewish garrison, your brother Hananiah. May God grant the prosperity of my brethren! Now, this year, the fifth year of King Darius [i.e., the second], word was sent by the King to Arsames: [gap in the text. . . .] Now you accordingly count fourteen days of the month Nisan and celebrate the Pasch, and from the fifteenth day to the twenty-first day of Nisan, celebrate the feast of the Azymes. Be clear and take heed! Do not work on the fifteenth or twenty-first day. Also do not drink beer [fermented drinks] and do not eat anything in which there is leaven; from the fifteenth day from sunset to the twenty-first day of Nisan, seven days, let it not be seen amongst you; do not bring it into your dwellings, but seal it up during those days.

What has happened to make the Persian king interested in Jewish ritual? It would seem that when Darius II

(424 B.C.) came to the throne, revolts broke out in many parts of the empire, and the king was made aware of the need for loyal supporters throughout the kingdom, even in its most distant parts. The Jews were chosen for this role for two reasons: on the one hand, Judaea provided an excellent military base in the vicinity of Egypt, and on the other, the Jews of the diaspora (that is, those living outside Palestine) would be faithful subjects, provided they were given some privileged treatment, however slight. Since their position would have to be legalised, the Persian officials probably turned to the Jewish law schools which now flourished in Babylon, and in which were preserved the doctrinal and legal traditions of Ezekiel and the priestly classes. This tradition strongly influenced the preparation of the statute which was to govern the worship of the Jews throughout the Empire, and give royal sanction to their liturgy.

The reform involved in this legislation was accomplished only gradually, and although in 419 B.C. it was well under way, it was still far from complete. In any event, the central administration probably devoted little time to the enforcement of new regulations in the remote community of Elephantine. All that Hananiah did was to notify his brethren concerning the paschal calendar used by the priestly scribes, and their manner of understanding the ritual of the Azymes. Authority is given to his recommendations by his appeal to the *royal decree* which had already been sent to Arsham, the satrap of Egypt.

This meagre papyrus from the ruins of Elephantine throws precious light on the history of the Pasch. From it we learn that the law of Deuteronomy was not universally imposed, although it was obligatory in Judaea; otherwise, Hananiah would not have tolerated the celebration of the Pasch outside Jerusalem. At the same time, it is clear that the priestly reforms were far advanced, because the regulations of Hananiah agree almost word for word with the priestly laws in our Pentateuch (Lev 23:5–8; Ex 12:15–20).

THE PASCHAL LAWS IN THEIR FINAL FORM

The paschal law soon received the final form in which it has come down to us. It sanctioned all the ancient law, both codified and customary, and by means of interpretative laws, sought to harmonise the differences, and even the contradictions, which distinguished the various traditions. This enormous work, which was of such importance for Judaism, is generally attributed to Ezra, who exercised his ministry some time in the latter half of the fifth century B.C.

Henceforth, all the ancient codes (the code of the covenant, the ritual decalogue, Deuteronomy), together with the traditions which served as their setting, are united in one legal *corpus* with the priestly legislation, which represents a parallel development. The priestly ritual for the Pasch (Ex 12:1–14) and the law of Deuteronomy, which reserved its celebration to the temple at Jerusalem (Deut 16:1–8), are both obligatory, and some additional regulations are added to forestall, or perhaps to put an end to, futile discussions. For example, the repose prescribed for the feast of the Azymes is less strict than the sabbath-day rest:

On these days you shall not do any sort of work, except to prepare the food that everyone needs (Ex 12:16).

The prohibition of leaven is further determined:

> From the evening of the fourteenth day of the first month until the evening of the twenty-first day of this month you shall eat unleavened bread. For seven days no leaven may be found in your houses. Anyone, be he a resident alien or a native, who eats leavened food shall be cut off from the community of Israel. Nothing leavened may you eat; wherever you dwell you may eat only unleavened bread (Ex 12:18–20).

This prohibition is now stiffened by a penalty of excommunication, and binds all Jews, whether in their homeland or in foreign countries. It adds the further detail: "On the very first day you shall remove all leaven from your houses" (Ex 12:15), and even today in Jewish families, the children are invited to search the whole house for crumbs of leavened bread which may have been overlooked. St. Paul had this in mind when he wrote to the Corinthians:

> Purge out the old leaven, that you may be a new dough, as you really are without leaven. For Christ, our Passover [Pasch], has been sacrificed. Therefore let us keep festival, not with the old leaven, nor with the leaven of malice and wickedness, but with the unleavened bread of sincerity and truth (1 Cor 5:7–8).

Not everyone may eat the Pasch:

> Yahweh said to Moses and Aaron, These are the regulations for the Passover. No foreigner may partake of it. However, any slave who has been bought for money may partake of it, provided you have first circumcised him. But no transient alien or hired servant may partake of it. It must be eaten in one and the same house; you may not take any of its flesh outside the house. You shall not break any of its bones [cf. Jn 19:36]. The whole

community of Israel must keep this feast. If any aliens living among you wish to celebrate the Passover of Yahweh, all the males among them must first be circumcised, and then they may join in its observance. But no man who is uncircumcised may partake of it. The law shall be the same for the resident alien as for the native (Ex 12:43–49).

The Pasch is therefore an act of faith. It is reserved to the people of Yahweh, of which one becomes a member by circumcision.[4] This exclusiveness is to be explained by the meaning of the feast: since it is the celebration of the first deliverance, it can only be appreciated by those who feel some solidarity with the Hebrews delivered by Yahweh. It foreshadows the supreme and final deliverance, but conveys this message only to those whom Yahweh has marked as his own. St. Paul recalls this promise: In Christ Jesus, "circumcision means nothing; the want of it means nothing; what is important is that one becomes a new creation" (Gal 6:15). All those whom Jesus Christ has marked with his seal in baptism will henceforward share in the new Pasch.

Finally, the celebration of the Pasch has become a serious obligation for a Jew, an obligation which raises problems concerning the obstacles which might prevent him from participating. He might, for example, be on a journey or have contracted a ritual impurity through contact with a dead person. For such cases, the law prescribed a second Pasch which was celebrated in the second month:

4. Judaism is not completely closed to outsiders, but if one wished to join it, one had to accept its beliefs and laws, including circumcision. Those who accepted these obligations and beliefs were known as "proselytes" (cf. Is 56:6–7).

There were some, however, who were unclean because of a human corpse [*cf.* Num 19:11] and so could not keep the Passover that day. These men came up to Moses and Aaron that same day and said, "Although we are unclean because of a corpse, why should we be deprived of presenting Yahweh's offering at its proper time along with the other Israelites?" Moses answered them, "Wait until I learn what Yahweh will command in your regard." Yahweh then said to Moses: "Speak to the Israelites and say: If any one of you or your descendants is unclean because of a corpse, or if he is absent on a journey, he may still keep Yahweh's Passover. But he shall keep it in the second month, during the evening twilight of the fourteenth day of that month, eating it with unleavened bread and bitter herbs, and not leaving any of it over till morning, nor breaking any of its bones, but observing all the rules of the Passover.

"However, anyone who is clean and not away on a journey, who yet fails to keep the Passover, shall be cut off from his people, because he did not present Yahweh's offering at the prescribed time. That man shall bear the consequences of his sin" (Num 9:6–13).

The Pasch is therefore a sign of belonging to the people of God. Excommunication is prescribed for those who fail to observe it and are not excused by law. In the course of time, however, it was admitted that in certain cases the journey to Jerusalem could be too difficult to undertake every year. Naturally, Jews living in Palestine would try to make it an annual pilgrimage. This was the custom of the holy family:

And his parents were wont to go every year to Jerusalem at the feast of the Passover. And when he was twelve years old, they went up to Jerusalem according to the custom of the feast (Lk 2:41–42).

From all sides they streamed into the holy city. Even in

the diaspora, the Jews felt obliged to make the journey as often as possible. Some remotely situated communities were unwilling to co-operate with the central authority, and continued to immolate the paschal lamb in exile. Some Jews in North Africa did so in the time of St. Augustine, as do the Jews of Ethiopia (Falashas) in our own day. The Samaritans still go in pilgrimage to celebrate the Pasch on Mount Gerizim where their temple once stood. They sacrifice the paschal lambs, which are eaten during the vigil feast which follows. These ceremonies have often been described by travellers in the holy land.

CHAPTER FIVE

The Pasch of Judaism

With Ezra, Judaism reaches its definitive form. Its law is now fixed, and on this basis, subsequent tradition will develop. It crystallises in various shapes, sometimes in inspired works—prophetical texts, psalms, books of wisdom, narrative, and apocalyse—sometimes in non-canonical writings, the oldest of which easily ante-date our own era, as well as in translations and explanations of the Scriptures. It is an immense literature at which we must cast a glance to complete the picture of the Pasch of our Lord.

THE JEWS CONTEMPLATE THE DELIVERANCE OF THE PAST

On reading the psalms, one is struck by the frequency with which memories of the exodus are revived. In days of trial, when the psalmist no longer understands the ways of God with men, when the sight of his suffering people brings the question to his lips: Will the Lord reject us forever? he recovers his faith and his courage while meditating the wonders of the past:

> O God, your way is holy;
>> what great god is there like our God?
> You are the God who works wonders;
>> among the peoples you have made known your power.
> With your strong arm you redeemed your people. . . .
>> (Ps 77(76):14–16a).

The sacred pages speak to us also of the patience of God who in spite of their frequent offences does not reject his people:

How often they rebelled against him in the desert
    and grieved him in the wilderness!
Again and again they tempted God
    and provoked the Holy One of Israel.
They remembered not his hand
    nor the day he delivered them from the foe,
When he wrought his signs in Egypt
    and his marvels in the plain of Zoan. . . .

[*Then follow the ten plagues*]

He smote every first-born in Egypt,
    the first fruits of manhood in the tents of Ham;
But his people he led forth like sheep
    and guided them like a herd in the desert
                  (Ps 78(77):40–43; 51–52).

The God of deliverance is also the God of mercy. Psalm 106 returns to this theme, when sorrow for a nation's sins leads to an earnest prayer:

Save us, O Yahweh, our God,
    and gather us from among the nations,
That we may give thanks to your holy name
    and glory in praising you (Ps 106(105): 47).

What God has done once, he can do again. One may read the story of his power in the fabric of Israel's history which is woven from the great deeds of Yahweh. Dominant amongst them is the exodus (Ps 105(104) and 114(113)), which comes second only to creation itself (Ps 136(135), which is called "the Great Hallel").

In each succeeding age, the same thought recurs; we find it in the Greek book, the Wisdom of Solomon (first century B.C.). Through long chapters (10–12; 16–19), the author, a Jew living in Egypt, compares the destinies reserved by God for his people and for the Egyptians: to the one, the divine intervention brought the light of his protecting cloud, to the other, the black darkness of rejection:

> That night was known beforehand to our fathers, . . .
> Your people awaited the salvation of the just and the
> destruction of their foes. For when you punished our
> adversaries, in this you glorified us whom you had
> summoned. For in secret the holy children of the good
> were offering sacrifice [i.e., the Pasch] and putting into
> effect with one accord the divine institution, that your
> holy ones should share alike the same good things and
> dangers, having previously sung the praises of the fathers.
> But the discordant cry of their enemies responded, and
> the piteous wail of mourning for children was borne to
> them. And the slave was smitten with the same retribu-
> tion as his master; even the plebian suffered the same as
> the king. And all together by a single death had countless
> dead. . . . For when peaceful stillness compassed every-
> thing and the night in its swift course was half spent,
> your all-powerful word from heaven's royal throne
> bounded, a fierce warrior, into the doomed land
> (Wis 18:6–15).

The flamboyant style of this text may well reflect the type of commentary which pleased the Jews of Egypt, when the Scriptures were explained to them in the synagogue. They never wearied of hearing the stories of their fathers, in which they loved to contemplate the pattern woven by divine providence, which in every age saves the just and "the saints."[1]

1. Perhaps it is not by chance that Wisdom 3:3 describes the death of the just as an exodus, a departure (Greek *exodos*). The same term

Let us now go back a little. The work of the Chronicler (that is, the author of the work which includes 1 and 2 Chronicles, Ezra and Nehemiah) is a reliable witness of Judaism towards the end of the fourth century B.C., about the time when the Samaritans broke away in schism. The author of this religious chronicle, which goes from Adam to Ezra and Nehemiah, is imbued with the doctrine and spirituality of the Pentateuch. He does not, however, write history in a spirit of scientific detachment; he is not motivated simply by that scientific curiosity which, it is claimed, alone impels modern historians when recovering and recording the past. No, he quite deliberately makes use of the words of his ancestors to demonstrate a thesis. This explains the freedom with which he treats his sources, especially the books of Samuel and Kings. He presumes that his readers are familiar with them and sets himself another purpose. He wishes to present his doctrinal teaching in the form of a continuous account of the past. He therefore omits the history of the northern kingdom of Israel after the schism between the north and south. The northern kingdom counted for nothing in his eyes, since its origin involved a break with the Davidic kingdom, and it could find no place in a work whose interest was focussed on the glories of the Davidic dynasty. His governing thought is that Yahweh has given to Israel a number of institutions centred around

---

occurs in Sirach 38:23; Luke 9:31; 2 Peter 1:15, and is used by St. Irenaeus to describe the death of Peter and Paul: "Mark wrote his gospel after the 'departure' (*exodos*) of Peter and Paul." The passage from this world to the next may be implicitly compared by these writers to the exodus of the Hebrews, but the word may just be a euphemism for death.

the throne of David and the temple at Jerusalem. For this reason, only the sanctuary which was built on the spot chosen by David and Solomon is a lawful place of worship. Only the Jews can expect the king, the son of David, who will realise the divine designs. Both points seem to be directed against the schismatic Samaritans, who had established a temple of their own, and claimed to be the heirs of the messianic promises. The Chronicler takes the same stand on this question as was taken by Christ in his conversation with the Samaritan woman: "Salvation is from the Jews" (Jn 4:22).

The work of the Chronicler, however, is not purely polemical; it includes also an appeal to unity. On two occasions the paschal feast provides the author with an opportunity for voicing such an appeal.

The fall of Samaria (722 B.C.) is not referred to in Chronicles, but it is presupposed in the account of Hezekiah's efforts to repair the unity of the people of God. In the first year of his reign, the king undertakes to reform religious life; he purifies the temple and restores the temple worship (2 Chron 29). He then invites all Judah and Israel to celebrate the Pasch. Since it is too late to celebrate the Pasch in the first month, he makes use of the law of the second Pasch, which we have already seen (Num 9:6 *ff.*):

> So they passed a decree to send a proclamation through-out all Israel, from Beer-sheba even to Dan, that they should come and keep the passover in honour of Yahweh, the God of Israel in Jerusalem; for they had not kept it in such great numbers, according to the record. So the couriers went with the letters from the king and his princes through all Israel and Judah, according to the command of the king, saying, "O Israelites! turn again

to Yahweh, the God of Abraham, Isaac, and Israel, that he may turn to the remnant which is left of you from the hand of the kings of Assyria. . . . For by your returning to Yahweh, your kinsmen and your sons shall find compassion in the presence of their captors so that they shall be allowed to return to this land; for Yahweh your God is gracious and merciful, and will not turn away his face from you if you return to him" (2 Chron 30:5-9).

These last lines of exhortation vibrate with the author's desire to see his wish fulfilled. If only they were faithful to Yahweh, if only they would celebrate his paschal feast as a sign of true conversion, then Yahweh would realise those promises whose fulfilment was so long in abeyance —the re-union of the scattered Jews for the inauguration of the messianic times. The narrative continues:

So the couriers passed from city to city through the land of Ephraim and Manasseh to Zebulun, but they laughed them to scorn and mocked them. Nevertheless some men from Asher and Manasseh and Zebulun humbled them-selves and came to Jerusalem. Also the hand of God was upon Judah to give them one heart, to do the bidding of the king and the princes by the word of Yahweh. So a great crowd of people assembled at Jerusalem to keep the feast of unleavened cakes in the second month. . . . They slaughtered the passover on the fourteenth day of the second month. . . .

So there was great joy in Jerusalem; for since the time of Solomon, the son of David, king of Israel, there had been nothing like this in Jerusalem. Then the priests and the Levites arose and blessed the people; and their voice was heard and their prayer came up to his holy habitation, even to the heavens (2 Chron 30:10-13, 15a, 26-27).

As in the gospel parable (Mt 22:2-14; Lk 14:16-24) many of those invited refused to come.

The Chronicler makes use of priestly traditions which were apparently not available to the deuteronomist scribes to whom we owe the books of Kings, for they make no mention of the great Pasch of Hezekiah. At the same time, we must not forget that he describes the past in terms of the realities of his own times. Those discourteous guests, those unfaithful Israelites who refuse to celebrate the Pasch at Jerusalem as the law demands, live in the territory of the former northern kingdom, in the province of Samaria. The faithful ones come for the most part from Judaea, a few from Galilee—a more or less accurate picture of Judaism at the end of the fourth century. The celebration of the Pasch as described by the Chronicler corresponds exactly to what he witnessed every year. He projects the picture into the past to underline the continuity of the living tradition of Israel.

The Chronicler addresses to the new separatists an appeal for unity. In his eyes the Pasch celebrated in common is the sign of unity. It is so even now. Christ is our Pasch: "Because the bread is one, we though many, are one body, all of us who partake of the one bread" (1 Cor 10:17).

This half-concealed wish of the Chronicler explains why he attributes great importance to the Pasch of Hezekiah. It happens just after the ruin of Samaria, at a time when the few who survived turned their steps towards Jerusalem, as we noted when speaking of Deuteronomy. The Chronicler, however, does not overlook the great Pasch of Josiah, which is already described in the second book of Kings (Chap 23). Once again, we have an accurate, though somewhat idealised picture of the Jewish liturgy in its definitive form. It helps us to visualise the paschal ceremonies in the temple in the time of our Lord:

> Then Josiah presented to the common people flocks, lambs, and kids—all of them for the passover offerings to all who were present, to the number of thirty thousand, and three thousand bulls, these being from the king's property. His princes also gave as a voluntary gift to the people, to the priests, and to the Levites. . . .
>
> So the service was established and the priests stood at their posts, and the Levites by their divisions, according to the king's command. Thus they slew the passover, and the priests sprinkled the blood from their hands, while the Levites skinned the victims. Then they removed the burnt-offerings that they might distribute them according to the divisions of the families of the common people, to offer to Yahweh. . . . Moreover they boiled the passover on the fire according to the ordinance, while they boiled the holy offerings in pots, in caldrons, and in pans, and carried them quickly to all the common people. Afterward they prepared some for themselves and for the priests. . . .
>
> The singers, the sons of Asaph, were at their posts . . . and the gate-keepers were at each gate; they had no need to depart from their service, for their kinsmen the Levites prepared it for them. So all the service of Yahweh was established the same day. . . . Thus the Israelites who were present kept the passover at that time and the feast of unleavened cakes seven days (2 Chron 35:7-8a, 10-17).

For the Chronicler, the Pasch is a feast which is celebrated in the temple, in an atmosphere of religious joy, the manifestation of which, however, was regulated by liturgical law.

Shortly after Josiah's Pasch, the nation met disaster; Jerusalem was taken and the temple destroyed (587 B.C.).

For the people of Yahweh, the years of exile and mourning dragged on, until with the decree of Cyrus (538 B.C.) they were free to return to Jerusalem. There they devoted their first energies to the rebuilding of the sanctuary and the restoration of worship (Ezra 1–3). The way was not easy; apart from the material obstacles, the Samaritans who should have helped, harassed and hindered them at every step (Ezra 4:1–6:18). At last, the temple was standing again. The Jews made a fresh start; as of old, they began with the paschal feast:

> Moreover the returned exiles kept the passover upon the fourteenth day of the first month. For the priests and the Levites had purified themselves to a man, all of them being ceremonially clean. They slaughtered the passover for all the returned exiles, both for their kinsmen the priests and for themselves. Then the Israelites who had returned from the captivity, and everyone who separated himself from the uncleanness of the peoples of the land to join them in order to seek Yahweh, the God of Israel, ate, and kept the feast of the unleavened cakes seven days with gladness; for Yahweh had made them joyful, and had turned the heart of the king of Persia to them, to strengthen their hands in the work of the house of God, the God of Israel (Ezra 6:19–22).

The Chronicler could not refrain from yet another slighting reference to the Samaritans ("the peoples of the land"), when describing this joyous festival which, while it recalls the first deliverance, marks the end of the exile and a new release. The Israelites now look forward to the final and everlasting deliverance.

WAITING FOR THE ETERNAL PASCH

The prophets, as we saw, described "the last days" as yet

81

another exodus. The author of the "apocalypse of Isaiah" (Is 24–27) goes even further. He seems to be thinking of the solemn celebration of the Pasch as the Chronicler described it, when he paints a picture of messianic joy in terms of a feast kept in the presence of God:

> On that day Yahweh will punish
>   the host of the heavens in the heavens,
> and the kings of the earth on the earth [cf. Ps 2]. . .
> Then the moon will blush
>   and the sun grow pale,
> For Yahweh of hosts will reign [cf. Is 52:7]
>   on Mount Zion and in Jerusalem [cf. Is 2:1–4],
>   glorious in the sight of his elders [cf. Ex 24:9–11].
> On this mountain Yahweh of hosts
>   will provide for all peoples
> A feast of rich food and choice wines,
>   juicy, rich food and pure, choice wines.
> On this mountain he will destroy
>   the veil that veils all peoples,
> The web that is woven over all nations;
>   he will destroy death forever [cf. Apoc 20:4].
> Yahweh God will wipe away
>   the tears from all faces [cf. Apoc 21:4];
> The reproach of his people he will remove
>   from the whole earth; for Yahweh has spoken.
> On that day it will be said:
> "Behold our God, to whom we looked to save us!
>   This is Yahweh for whom we looked;
>   let us rejoice and be glad that he has saved us!"
>
> (Is 24:21 and 23; 25:6–9).

This sacred banquet to which all men are invited recalls not only the Pasch but also the feast of the covenant, which was eaten on Sinai in the presence of Yahweh by the elders who accompanied Moses (Ex 24:9–11). These two themes of the Pasch and the covenant (testament) are re-united in the perspective of the "last times," as we shall see happening at the Last Supper.

The passage just quoted refers to wine, which is not explicitly mentioned in the ancient ritual. When the book of Jubilees (second century B.C.) describes the exodus, it transfers the ritual of its own time to the past in saying:

> All the Israelites ate the flesh of the paschal lamb *and drank wine*, and praised and blessed and gave thanks to the God of their fathers, and prepared themselves to pass under the yoke of Egypt and slavery to evil (Jubilees 49:16).

Other texts show that during the same period, the gathering of the elect in the messianic times was likened to the massing of the pilgrim crowds as they made their way up to Mount Zion. A sample is to be found in the Greek translation of Jeremiah. The translator found the following Hebrew text:

> For thus says Yahweh:
> Shout with joy for Jacob,
> exult at the head of the nations;
> proclaim your praise and say:
> Yahweh has delivered his people,
> the remnant of Israel.
> Behold, I will bring them back
> from the land of the north;
> I will gather them from the ends of the world,
> with the blind and the lame in their midst,
> The mothers and those with child;
> they shall return as an immense throng.
> They departed in tears,
> but I will console them and guide them;
> I will lead them to brooks of water,
> on a level road, so that none shall stumble.
> For I am a father to Israel,
> Ephraim is my first-born (Jer 31:7–9).

The Greek translator, working in the second century B.C., did not simply translate the text; he interpreted it, and introduced a reference to the paschal feast in this description of the last times:

> Behold I will bring them from the north country
> I will gather them from the ends of the earth
> *In a paschal feast* (Jer 31:8 [Greek Version]).

ON THAT NIGHT THE MESSIAH WILL COME

The Jews continued to live in expectation of the eternal Pasch, and their hope was quickened by the annual celebration of the paschal vigil. A proverb found in an old rabbinical work says:

> On that night they were saved
> And on that night they shall be saved.

As a final witness to this period, we shall quote the Aramaic translation or Targum of the Pentateuch, which incorporates an ancient poem on the same theme. To avoid speaking directly of Yahweh, the Jewish doctors referred to the "Memra of Yahweh," that is, "the creative word of Yahweh," when describing God's creative and saving activity, as can be seen in the following passage:

> Four nights are written in the Book of Memories.
> The first night:
>> When the Memra of Yahweh revealed himself to the world by creating it. . . .
> The second night:
>> When the Memra of Yahweh revealed himself to Abraham between the divided animals. . . . (*cf.* Gen 15)
> The third night:
>> When the Memra of Yahweh revealed himself to the Egyptians at midnight.

With one hand he slew the first-born of the Egyptians,
With the other he saved the first-born of Israel
to accomplish what the Scripture says:
"Israel is my first-born."
The fourth night:
When the world shall come to an end
That the Deliverance may be accomplished.
The bonds of iniquity shall be broken
The yokes of iron shall be shattered
Moses shall come from the midst of the desert
And the Messiah from the middle of Rome.[2]
One shall advance on the crest of a cloud.
The other shall advance on the crest of a cloud
And the Memra of Yahweh shall advance in between
And they shall go together.
Such is the night of the Pasch, a night of vigil
established by Yahweh for all Israel.

(Targum Yerushalmi 11 on Exodus 12,42)

These texts throw light on the rather obscure words of
Jesus at the beginning of the Last Supper:

And when the hour had come, he reclined at table, and
the twelve apostles with him. And he said to them, "I
have greatly desired to eat this passover with you before
I suffer; for I say to you that I will eat of it no more,
until it has been fulfilled in the kingdom of God."
And having taken a cup, he gave thanks and said, "Take
this and share it among you; for I say to you that I will
not drink of the fruit of the vine, until the kingdom of
God comes" (Lk 22:14–18).

2. Moses comes from the desert because he was buried there (Deut
34). The messiah comes from Rome, which was the capital of the
pagan world. Jewish belief at the time expected that the messiah would
spend the first years of his life there and would even begin his messianic
activities amongst the pagans of Rome, just as Moses had begun
among the Egyptians.

Or even more clearly in St. Mark:

I will drink no more of the fruit of the vine, until that day when I shall drink it new in the kingdom of God (Mk 14:25).

Our minds go back to the scene in the apocalypse of Isaiah. The messiah has come and the glory of the kingdom of God is at hand. By his death, Jesus will enter into it, the first of many brethren, because he will go to prepare a place for us. The ancient Pasch, celebrated for the last time by Jesus, loses none of its meaning. Soon it will be succeeded by the new Pasch, the eternal Pasch, whose sacrament and sign the Lord will bequeath to his apostles.

We
have a duty
to thank, to sing, to praise, to glorify,
to exalt, to celebrate, to bless,
to magnify, to honour
Him
who has wrought these great miracles
for our ancestors
and for us.
He has led us
from slavery to liberty, from distress to peace,
from mourning to joy, from darkness to light,
from servitude to independence.
Let us sing in his honour:
ALLELUIA!
—*Ritual of the Jewish Pasch*

PART II

The Pasch in the New Testament

The Feast in the New Testament

Prologue

It is in terms of the paschal themes with which you are now familiar that the mysteries of the final redemption are revealed to us in the New Testament. They occur first of all in the preaching of Jesus, but it is in the accounts of the Last Supper and the institution of the new paschal feast that they are given the greatest prominence. The relevant texts are to be found in the first three gospels and in St. Paul.

Christian thought from the epistles to the Apocalypse frequently returns to the subject of "Christ Our Pasch," and leads up to the fourth gospel, which orders the whole ministry of Jesus around three paschal feasts. Christ is, for St. John, the *lamb of God*, who on the cross bears the sins of the world and inaugurates the final exodus to lead us from the captivity of this world to the Father.

You are now equipped to understand the numerous references in the New Testament to the mysteries of the Jewish Pasch. A few words of guidance, however, will not be out of place, as you study what the New Testament tells us about the new and eternal Pasch.

CHAPTER SIX

Towards the Christian Pasch

THE BOY JESUS AT THE PASCHAL FEAST

When he was but twelve years old, Jesus went to Jerusalem with his parents to take part in the celebration of the Pasch (Lk 2:41–42). Luke's account of the incident is so brief as to seem almost laconic. He tells us that Jesus remained behind in Jerusalem while his parents sought him in sorrow, and they eventually found him amongst the doctors, who taught in the temple porches,

> listening to them and asking them questions (Lk 2:46).

> When your children ask you, "What does this rite of yours mean?" you shall reply, "This is the Passover sacrifice of Yahweh, who passed over the houses of the Israelites in Egypt; when he struck down the Egyptians, he spared our houses" (Ex 12:26–27).

"Jesus *asks*." The paschal feast which had just ended may have stirred the child's curiosity, and brought to his lips many a question on rite and ritual, on symbol and meaning. For answer, the doctors could draw on the wealth of tradition which had grown from the sacred text. Jesus wishes to inherit the riches of Jewish tradition which are his right as a member of the Jewish race. With a growing understanding, his heart will throb in unison with his people when they celebrate their national feasts. Every year he will share in their paschal joy, and as he does so, he will realise that the final act of the divine drama in which he plays the leading role will be enacted on the paschal scene. His glorious but formidable destiny is none other than to "accomplish" the Pasch in all its fullness. This first Pasch of Jesus Christ foreshadows in a mysterious way the last, and everlasting, paschal feast.

JESUS ANNOUNCES THE NEW EXODUS

Jesus has just begun his public life. The scene is set in the synagogue of Nazareth on a sabbath day (Lk 4:16-21). The congregation has assembled and awaits the reading and instruction. Jesus, the carpenter, mounts the pulpit; he unrolls the text of Isaiah and reads:

The spirit of Yahweh God is upon me,
    because Yahweh has anointed me;
he has sent me to bring glad tidings to the lowly,
    to heal the brokenhearted,
    to proclaim liberty to the captives
    and release to the prisoners,
to announce a year of favour from Yahweh
    and a day of vindication by our God (Is 61:1-2).

In the book of Isaiah this text referred to the return of the Jews from exile and the restoration of Mount Zion. What meaning will Christ now give to it? As he rolls up the book and hands it to the attendant, the eyes of all are upon him. Will he simply draw on what he has learned from tradition, invite his hearers to continued hope, and, as encouragement, paint glowing pictures of the messianic times? No, Jesus has another message for his hearers:

Today this Scripture has been fulfilled in your hearing (Lk 4:21).

On Christ's own testimony, this text, this "scripture," defines his sacred mission. It is he who has been sent to proclaim "the good tidings," the "good spell," the *evangelium*. The text concerns his hearers too, for it is to them that he addresses his message of joy.

The "good news," the gospel, which he has begun to preach, is not only the gospel of the kingdom of God, it is the gospel of deliverance, of freedom restored, the gospel of the new exodus promised by the prophets. In this exodus, Jesus himself will be the paschal lamb, a fact which is hidden from the people. To his most cherished disciples Christ reveals it but gradually, and even they will only understand it fully when he celebrates the last Pasch in their midst.

THE LAST PASCH OF JESUS

It was at the Last Supper that Christ inaugurated the new Pasch and for the last time ate the ancient Pasch in the company of his apostles. The events are described in varying detail by the first three evangelists and by Paul. Their accounts become clearer when we recall what the books of the Old Testament teach us about the Pasch. Jewish tradition, too, has much to tell us about the celebration of the paschal supper in the time of Christ.

The psalms of praise, sung during the meal, will give the true meaning of the gestures of Christ, and will recapture for us the sentiments which were his in these dramatic moments.

1. *The Approach of the Azymes.*

Now it was two days before the Passover and the feast of the Unleavened Bread; the chief priests and the Scribes were seeking how they might seize him by stealth and put him to death; for they said, "Not on the feast, or there might be a riot among the people" (Mk 14:1–2).

Jesus is not deceived:

> You know that after two days the Passover will be here; and the Son of Man will be delivered up to be crucified (Mt 26:2).

The shadow of approaching death descends upon the last Pasch of Jesus. The day he utters these words he is at Bethany near Jerusalem, in the house of Simon the leper. During the meal a woman anoints his feet with perfumed ointment:

> But Jesus said, "Let her be. Why do you trouble her? She has done me a good turn. . . ." (Mk 14:3–9; Mt 26: 6–13).

Shortly afterwards, it would appear, Judas Iscariot made his offer to the chiefs of the priests (Mk 14:10–11; Mt 26:14–16; Lk 22:3–6). The atmosphere of these last days was heavy with doom, as the little circle of disciples clung ever more closely to the master, in whom they found refuge from uncertainty and fear.

2. *The Paschal Supper.*

And on the first day of the Unleavened Bread, when it was customary for them to sacrifice the passover, the disciples said to him, "Where dost thou want us to go and prepare for thee to eat the passover?" And he sent two of his disciples, and said to them, "Go into the city, and there will meet you a man carrying a pitcher of water; follow him. And wherever he enters, say to the master of the house, 'The Master says, "Where is my guest chamber, that I may eat the passover there with my disciples?"' And he will show you a large upper room

furnished; there make ready for us." And his disciples
went forth, and came into the city, and found just as he
had told them; and they prepared the passover (Mk 14:
12–16).

When the evangelists speak of preparing for the Pasch,
they imply the search for the old leaven—hidden perhaps
in odd corners of the house—the arrangement of the
room where the meal will take place, the provision of
cushions for the guests, the purchase of the necessary
foodstuffs and the ritual immolation of the lamb in the
temple at the time prescribed by the law.

And when the hour had come, he reclined at table, and
the twelve apostles with him (Lk 22:14).

A detailed description of the paschal supper is given in
the tract of the Mishna entitled *Pesachim*. Since this
rabbinical text dates from the latter half of the second
century A.D., some modifications may have been introduced since the time of Christ, but they would concern
unimportant details. One may therefore use this source
to reconstruct the paschal supper as celebrated by Christ,
and to clear up obscure references in the gospel narratives,
which are exceedingly brief, and little interested in
ceremonial which ceased to be obligatory for Christians.
It is for this reason that the gospel accounts of the Last
Supper make no reference to the paschal lamb.

They had hardly entered the upper room when Jesus
said to his disciples:

I have greatly desired to eat this passover with you before
I suffer; for I say to you that I will eat of it no more,
until it has been fulfilled in the kingdom of God (Lk 22:
15–16).

Although the thought of his sufferings weighed heavily upon him, Christ reached out from his present sorrow and revealed to his apostles a future which was full of hope and consolation. This was to be the last Pasch of the old law; the eschatological Pasch of the kingdom of God would follow, and Israel need wait no longer.

The ceremony began with the blessing of the first cup, a prayer which called down a blessing on the wine. . . . Then herbs were brought in with a dishful of sauce. The Jews were acquainted with the use of forks, but on this occasion, they used their fingers, dipping the herbs into the sauce. When this course was finished the paschal lamb was placed on the table, and a commemoration was made of the mercies of God. The head of the family explained the reason for which they were performing this rite, recalling the deliverance of Israel. No strict formula was prescribed, though the Mishna suggests the subjects to be spoken of, after the manner of our own homiletical works. The second cup was drunk and the lamb eaten along with bitter herbs. . . .

It was not forbidden to introduce other foods into this paschal meal, such as eggs, or even other meats which had been offered in sacrifice in the Temple. After the eating of the lamb, a third cup was poured out and an act of thanksgiving was offered. The fourth cup is mentioned immediately afterwards, being followed by the hymn "Hallel," which was composed of Psalms 113:8–18 and 114–117.[1]

At the first cup, Jesus resumes the thought with which he entered:

And having taken a cup, he gave thanks and said, "Take this and share it among you; for I say to you that I will not drink of the fruit of the vine, until the kingdom of God comes" (Lk 22:17–18).

1. M. J. Lagrange, O.P., *The Gospel of Jesus Christ*, Vol. II, pp. 197–198.

On reading these words, one's first impression is of a vow of abstinence, but the words in fact announce the end of the ancient Pasch and the approach of the feast at which Jesus "will drink new wine in the kingdom of God" (Mk 14:25).

Newness is characteristic of all that concerns the kingdom; the covenant which inaugurates it is a new covenant (Lk 22:20); its doctrine is new (Mk 1:27); its members are new creatures (2 Cor 5:7; Gal 6:16): it involves the renewal of all things in God (Apoc 21:5). In this transcendent kingdom of God, a new wine will be served, a wine which will eternally refresh, and give to the members of the kingdom a joy which their eyes have not seen, nor their ears heard, nor their hearts ever conceived (1 Cor 2:9). It is on this glowing horizon that Christ fixes his gaze as the clouds of sorrow thicken about him.

The evangelists are silent on the subject of the paschal lamb, probably because it had no place in Christian ritual. Neither do they tell us how Jesus, as master of the household, explained the meaning of the feast. The words just quoted give the trend of his discourse. They were not merely a repetition of the ancient traditions he had learned to know and love, for they drew attention to the place his death would have in the inauguration of the new and eternal Pasch. The deliverance and redemption of mankind would depend on the death of the lamb of God.

And while they were at the table eating, Jesus said, "Amen I say to you, one of you will betray me—one who is eating with me." But they began to be sad, and to say to him one by one, "Is it I?" But he said to them,

"It is one of the Twelve, who dips into the dish with me. The Son of Man indeed goes his way, as it is written of him; but woe to that man by whom the Son of Man is betrayed! It were better for that man if he had not been born" (Mk 14:18–21, *cf.* Mt 26:20–24).

And while they were at supper, Jesus took bread, and blessed and broke and gave it to his disciples, and said, "Take and eat; this is my body" (Mt 26:26).

The fourth gospel tells how Jesus pointed out the traitor to Peter and John by giving him a morsel dipped in sauce. This happened during the first course:

When therefore, he had received the morsel, he went out quickly. Now it was night (Jn 13:30).

3. *The Azymes Become the Body of Christ.*

And while they were eating, Jesus took bread, and blessing it, he broke and gave it to them and said, "Take; this is my body" (Mk 14:22).

And while they were at supper, Jesus took bread, and blessed and broke, and gave it to his disciples, and said, "Take and eat; this is my body" (Mt 26:26).

Paul's account adds a detail or two:

The Lord Jesus, on the night in which he was betrayed, took bread, and giving thanks broke, and said, "This is my body which shall be given up for you; do this in remembrance of me" (1 Cor 11:23–24).

In Luke we read:

And having taken bread, he gave thanks and broke, and gave it to them saying, "This is my body, which is being given for you; do this in remembrance of me" (Lk 22:19).

They had come to the central point of the paschal

supper. With moving solemnity, Jesus carries out the sacred gestures prescribed by the Jewish ritual, on which he grafts the sacramental rites of the new liturgy.

The documents discovered near the Dead Sea in recent years include a rule of life for a religious community to which these documents apparently belonged. This rule throws light on the ancient paschal ritual when it describes the procedure at the banquet to be celebrated when the messiah shall come. The priest of the community shall take precedence over the messiah at the feast, because the priesthood ranks higher than the laity:

> When they shall meet at the common table or to drink wine, and the common table has been set and the wine mixed for drinking, let no one put out his hand for the first piece of bread or the wine before the priest; for it belongs to him to bless the first piece of bread and the wine, and to put out his hand for bread first of all. Afterwards the Messiah of Israel shall put out his hands for bread, and then the whole assembled community shall utter a blessing, each according to his rank.
>
> In accordance with this prescription shall they act at every meal for which at least ten men have come together.

The last phrase refers to the meal of the brotherhood, for which it prescribes the ceremonial.

More than once Jesus would have followed similar customs when eating with his disciples. They were accustomed to see him bless the bread and wine and take the first portion. But the mysterious words spoken on this occasion give to the simple gesture of the breaking of bread an overwhelming importance:

> This is my body *which is delivered for you.*

Christ undoubtedly refers to his approaching death, a death which is no mere accident which Jesus happens to foresee. It is a ritual sacrifice of which he is the priest and victim, a sacrifice of substitution in which his body is offered for his own people to expiate their sins (Is 53:10).

The thoughts and the actions of Christ pass beyond the limits of the annual Pasch, but the requirements of the ancient ritual—the paschal lamb, recently slain, the unleavened bread, the herbs—provide the setting and a link with the past.

> Take ye and eat: This is my body.

With these words Jesus institutes a new paschal meal, in which the body of the Lord is eaten under the appearances of bread.

4. *The Blood of the New Testament.* The third cup followed the meal. While it was being poured one gave thanks to God by starting to chant the Hallel (Psalms 113(112)–114(113a):

> In like manner also the cup, after he had supped, saying, "This cup is the new covenant in my blood; do this as often as you drink it, in remembrance of me" (1 Cor 11:25).

Jesus here establishes a new memorial. His words are recorded by the evangelists with slight variations:

> This cup is the new covenant in my blood, which shall be shed for you (Lk 22:20).

> This is my blood of the new covenant, which is being shed for many (Mk 14:24).

> All of you drink of this; for this is my blood of the new covenant, which is being shed for many unto the forgiveness of sins (Mt 26:27–28).

Many strands of tradition are here drawn together: the blood of the paschal lamb which was sprinkled on the doors to ensure the safety of the Hebrews; the blood of the victims with which was concluded the covenant on Mount Sinai (Ex 24:4-8); the blood of the sacrifices which were offered for men's sins (Lev 16:14 ff.); and finally the expiation offered for the multitudes by the "servant of Yahweh" (Is 53:10-11). The dominating themes of the Old Testament revelation are united in the paschal meal of Jesus: deliverance, covenant, expiation, all those different aspects of the promised redemption, just as they are presented side by side in the second part of Isaiah (40-55). In the cenacle, "the servant of Yahweh" is present (Is 53). He goes to his death "as it is written of him" (Mt 26:24), but by his death he "fulfills the Scriptures" (Mt 26:54) and saves us (Is 53:11-12; cf. Ps 22(21):26-32). He puts God's seal on the prophetic promises (Lk 22:37). The new exodus will shortly begin, and the right of deliverance and salvation will be purchased by the blood of the new paschal lamb.

5. *Songs of Deliverance.* The paschal ritual mentions a fourth cup which is poured soon after the third. Then the singing of the "Hallel" (Ps 114(113a)-118(117)) is continued. The origin of these songs and their original liturgical setting are here of little importance. By reason of the fact that they were sung during the paschal vigil, they were brought into an immediate relationship with the objects of the feast. The first part of the Hallel concludes with the paschal hymn of Psalm 114(113a):

When Israel came forth from Egypt,
   the house of Jacob from a people of alien tongue,
Judah became his sanctuary,
   Israel his domain (Ps 114(113a):1-2).

It was, therefore, to the *God of deliverance* that Israel sang on that day:

> Not to us, O Yahweh, not to us
>   but to your name give glory
>   because of your kindness, because of your truth.
> Why should the pagans say,
>   "Where is their God?"
> Our God is in heaven;
>   whatever he will, he does. . . .
> The house of Israel trusts in Yahweh;
>   he is their help and their shield, . . .
> It is not the dead who praise Yahweh,
>   nor those who go down into silence;
>
> (Ps 115(113b):1–3, 9, 17).

Did not God revive his people after the exile (Ezek 37), and confirm the trust they had put in their God?

To Israel, God's chosen people, is applied the thanksgiving song of a man who has been snatched by God from the jaws of death:

> I love Yahweh because he has heard
>   my voice in supplication,
> Because he has inclined his ear to me
>   the day I called.
> The cords of death encompassed me;
>   the snares of the nether world seized upon me;
> I fell into distress and sorrow,
> And I called upon the name of Yahweh,
>   "O Yahweh, save my life!"
>
> Gracious is Yahweh and just;
>   yes, our God is merciful.
> Yahweh keeps the little ones;
>   I was brought low and he saved me (Ps 116(114):1–6).

He saved Israel from Egypt. Through the ages, he saved those who trusted in him. . . . When Jesus sang

these words with his disciples in the cenacle, a new
salvation, another resurrection, was being prepared. It
was the definitive redemption, paid for with his blood,
which would inaugurate his victory over death. The
disciples must surely have grasped, at least in a confused
way, the import of what was happening. A new perspective was revealed in words which were still shrouded
in mystery when they spoke of the "chalice of the *New*
Testament," and in actions which brought to their lips
the blood which gives life everlasting (Jn 6:55):

> How shall I make a return to Yahweh
>   for all the good he has done for me?
> The cup of salvation I will take up,
>   and I will call upon the name of Yahweh;
>   (Ps 116:12–13(115:3–4)).

The *cup of blessing* of the paschal meal has indeed
become the *cup of salvation*, a change of which the early
Christians were keenly aware, when they celebrated the
eucharist in memory of the Lord:

> The cup of blessing that we bless, is it not the sharing of
> the blood of Christ? And the bread that we break, is it
> not the partaking of the body of the Lord? (1 Cor 10:16).

These few words of Paul reflect the dramatic trans-
formation of the Jewish rites which have been retained
in the Christian liturgy. The gestures are the same; some
of the texts remain unchanged; the same psalms accompany the celebration of the Pasch, old and new. In
reality, however, all is changed; the sacrifice of Jesus, the
source of resurrection and life, is the only reality which is
present under those ancient signs, which for so long had
foreshadowed its coming.

The Hallel continues:

Praise Yahweh, all you nations;
    glorify him, all you peoples! (Ps 117(116):1).

Alleluia!

Give thanks to Yahweh, for he is good,
    for his mercy endures forever (Ps 118(117):1).

Jesus and his apostles are standing. Outside it is night.
The scene for the passion is being set. Jesus knows, but is
full of confidence:

Yahweh is with me; I fear not;
    what can man do against me? . . .

My strength and my courage is Yahweh,
    and he has been my savior.

The joyful shout of victory
    in the tents of the just;
"The right hand of Yahweh has struck with power;
    the right hand of Yahweh is exalted;
    the right hand of Yahweh has struck with power"
                            (Ps 118(117):6,14–16).

These "voices" re-echo the chants which greeted the
great deliverance on the banks of the Red Sea:

Your right hand, O Yahweh, magnificent in power,
    your right hand, O Yahweh, has shattered the enemy
                            (Ex 15:6).

Jesus does not falter, as he goes to his death. What had
he to fear from men? God is stronger than they, for he
is the God of deliverance.

I shall not die, but live,
    and declare the works of Yahweh.

Though Yahweh has indeed chastised me,
    yet he has not delivered me to death.
Open to me the gates of justice;
    I will enter them and give thanks to Yahweh
                        (Ps 118(117):17–19).

"I shall not die but live." These words of triumphant assurance draw light through the portals of death. Suffering is but the gateway to glory:

The stone which the builders rejected
    has become the cornerstone.
By Yahweh has this been done;
    it is wonderful in our eyes (Ps 118(117):22–23).

It was not long since Jesus had spoken to the priests the parable of the vineyard:

But the vine-dressers said to one another, "This is the heir; come, let us kill him, and the inheritance will be ours." So they seized him and killed him, and cast him out of the vineyard (Mk 12:7–8).

He was telling the story of his own decease, but all would not end with his death; it would have a sequel:

And have you not read this Scripture: "The stone which the builders rejected, has become the corner stone" (Mk 12:10).

6. *The Day of the Lord.* On that paschal evening, the thought of final triumph gave courage to the heart of Christ, as he led his people from bondage:

This is the day which Yahweh has made;
    let us be glad and rejoice in it.
O Yahweh, grant salvation!
    O Yahweh, grant prosperity!
Blessed is he who comes in the name of Yahweh;
    we bless you from the house of Yahweh
                        (Ps 118(117):24–26).

A few days before, on the slopes which lead to the holy city, an enthusiastic crowd had wildly acclaimed its messiah:

> And many spread their cloaks upon the road, while others were cutting branches from the trees, and strewing them on the road. And those who went before him, and those who followed, kept crying out, saying,
>
> "Hosanna!
> Blessed is he who comes in the name of Yahweh!
> Blessed is the kingdom of our father David
>   that comes!
> Hosanna in the highest!" (Mk 11:8–10).

Jesus had no illusions about this passing triumph: "The son of man must suffer before he enters into his glory" (*cf.* Lk 24:26). First, he must be taken from his own. He had said so himself:

> For I say to you, ye shall not see me henceforth until ye say: "Blessed is he that comes in the name of the Lord."

The hour of his glory is at hand; Jesus speaks of it to the eleven, when the hymn has been sung:

> But you are they who have continued with me in my trials. And I appoint to you a kingdom, even as my Father has appointed to me, that you may eat and drink at my table in my kingdom; and you shall sit upon thrones, judging the twelve tribes of Israel (Lk 22: 28–30).

He directs their thoughts to the messianic banquet (Is 25:6; *cf.* also Mt 8:11–12; Lk 13:28–29), of which the eucharistic banquet is a proclamation, a promise, and an anticipation. With good reason, therefore, does Jesus sing his Hallel of victory in the cenacle, for in his duel with death, it is he who shall triumph:

For as often as you shall eat this bread and drink the cup, you proclaim the death of Yahweh, until he comes (1 Cor 11:26).

Henceforth, whenever the Christian puts the cup of salvation to his lips, he looks forward more earnestly to the return of his Lord.

For as often as you shall eat this bread and drink the cup, you proclaim the death of ... (until he comes) (1 Cor 11:26).

... Whoever is faithful will ... ... salvation to his ... He looks forward more earnestly to the return of his Lord.

CHAPTER SEVEN

Christ, Our Pasch

"Christ, our passover, has been sacrificed" (1 Cor 5:7). This cry resounds triumphantly on the lips of Paul, for it was by the immolation of this victim that our deliverance was effected. Each time the eucharist is celebrated, it recalls and prolongs the Last Supper of Jesus. Each year brings the anniversary of its institution in the spring, and with it a special remembrance of the events which accompanied it. They are re-presented to-day in the paschal liturgy, just as was done in the days of Paul in a less developed form (1 Cor 5:7–8).

For the Jews, this anniversary is the occasion for celebrating "the feast," the great night of vigil with seven days of Azymes to follow; it carries the promise of final salvation. The Christians know that salvation has come, for Christ, their Pasch, has been immolated once for all (Rom 6:10). Like their fathers, they have passed from bondage to freedom (1 Cor 10:1–13; Heb 3:7–4:10), from death to life, from darkness to light (Col 1:12*f*). Grace has given them new life and the annual feast invites them to live by faith in this mystery:

> Purge out the old leaven, that you may be a new dough, as you really are without leaven. For Christ, our passover, has been sacrificed. Therefore let us keep festival, not with the old leaven nor with the leaven of malice and wickedness, but with the unleavened bread of sincerity and truth (1 Cor 5:7–8).

The text of Paul suggests that the new Pasch involves Christ and Christians together, for the Christians make with Christ but "one body"; with him, they have become immolated victims, and pure, unleavened bread:

> Therefore beloved, flee from the worship of idols. I am speaking as to men of sense; judge for yourselves what I say. The cup of blessing that we bless, is it not the sharing of the blood of Christ? And the bread that we break, is it not the partaking of the body of the Lord? Because the bread is one, we though many, are one body, all of us who partake of the one bread (1 Cor 10:14–17).

THE PASCH IN APOSTOLIC TIMES

The epistles and the Acts of the Apostles give surprisingly little information about the manner in which the early Christians celebrated the paschal feast. The Acts of the Apostles (12:1–17) show us the Christians assembled in the house of Mark's mother during the Azymes. Peter had been thrown into prison by Herod, who intended "to bring him forth to the people after the Pasch." This is the only reference to the Pasch in the Acts. There is also the briefest mention of the Azymes in Acts 20:6 where it is said that Paul, during his third journey, embarked at Philippi "after the days of the Azymes."

Such scant notice, however, should not obscure the fact that the "Lord's supper" (1 Cor 11:20) was celebrated with special solemnity on the anniversary of the Pasch, as is witnessed by the subsequent development of the paschal liturgy.

Perhaps in those early days, the celebration of the eucharist on the paschal feast was accompanied by instruction concerning its origin and meaning. Where the Jewish father had recalled for his children the intervention of Yahweh to save his people, Paul reminds the Corinthians of the words and actions of Jesus which make the Christian Pasch new, and give it its meaning (1 Cor 11:23-35). Indeed other passages of his first letter to the Corinthians may have formed part of this paschal instruction (cf. 1 Cor 10:1-13; 15:3-56 and 1 Cor 5:7).

The public reading of the passion and resurrection story would early become a feature of the paschal liturgy, and would find a place beside the account of the exodus as read by the Jews. Perhaps Paul refers to this practice when he writes:

> For as often as you shall eat this bread and drink the cup, you *proclaim the death of the Lord*, until he comes (1 Cor 11:26).

These are not mere suppositions, for the liturgy of holy week has developed precisely along those lines, and liturgies, in general, are conservative. We have seen already how the Jewish Pasch retained until Roman times—and retains even to-day—rites which go back to the nomadic life of the thirteenth century B.C. and earlier.

Whatever may be said about the origin of certain details of the Christian feast, the death of Christ, our Pasch, was never divorced from his resurrection, nor his resurrection from the death on the cross. They are but two aspects of the same mystery—suffering and glory—two facets of the same life which was lived and laid down that the grace of salvation might be ours.

> Jesus was delivered up for our sins, and rose again for our justification (Rom 4:25).

The Pasch of Christ, the mystery of death and resurrection, is for each Christian the source of a new life to which he is born in baptism, and which, in grace, he continues to live. It is not surprising, therefore, to find the solemn administration of baptism occupying a prominent place in the liturgy of Easter, and the grace of baptism is often referred to in terms which recall the paschal deliverance. Peter reminds the "newly-born" in baptism whence their new life is derived:

> You know that you were redeemed from the vain manner of life handed down from your fathers, not with perishable things, with silver or gold, but with the precious blood of Christ, as of a lamb without blemish and without spot. Foreknown, indeed, before the foundation of the world, he has been manifested in the last times for your sakes (1 Pet 1:18-20).

His thoughts are re-echoed in the sequence of the Mass for Easter Sunday:

> Christians,
> so the paschal Victim offer your thankful
> praises.
> The lamb the sheep redeemeth:
> Christ, who only is sinless,
> reconcileth sinners to the Father.

CHAPTER EIGHT

The Eternal Pasch

THE APOCALYPSE

At the beginning of the Apocalypse we read:

> I, John, your brother and partner in the tribulation and
> kingdom and patience that are in Jesus, was on the island
> which is called Patmos, because of the word of God and
> the testimony of Jesus. I was in the spirit on the Lord's
> day . . . (Apoc 1:9–10).

Sunday, the Lord's day, has become for Christians
the day of worship, because on that day, Jesus, the lamb
of the new Pasch, was raised from the dead. Sunday is,
in a sense, our weekly Pasch. It was apparently on this
day that John beheld God enthroned amongst the twenty-
four elders. Four symbolic animals stood by. In his right
hand, God held a mysterious book, sealed with seven
seals, which none could open or read. Before the throne
stood a lamb, which was slain, yet lived:

> And I saw, and behold, in the midst of the throne, and
> of the four living creatures, and in the midst of the elders,
> a Lamb standing, as if slain, having seven horns and
> seven eyes, which are the seven spirits of God sent forth
> into all the earth. And he came and took the scroll out
> of the right hand of him who sat upon the throne. And
> when he had opened the scroll, the four living creatures
> and the twenty-four elders fell down before the Lamb,
> having each a harp and golden bowls full of incense,

which are the prayers of the saints. And they sing a new canticle, saying:

"Worthy art thou to take the scroll
    and to open its seals;
For thou wast slain, and hast re-
    deemed us
for God with thy blood,
Out of every tribe and tongue and people
    and nation,
And hast made them for our God a kingdom
    and priests,
And they shall reign over the earth" (Apoc 5:6–10).

The lamb is master of history; he knows its meaning; in fact, it was his sacrifice that gave it its meaning. From the multitude of races, of tongues and of nations (Gen 11:1–9) shall emerge the new people, the race redeemed, the priestly kingdom, the holy nation (Ex 19:6) without which the unfolding of the ages has no meaning. As it grows towards perfection, it must live in continual conflict. To such a life was the infant Church born of the new Pasch, yet she carries on the struggle with confidence, for God is at her side; he has come in person to save his holy ones.

The elaborate imagery of the Apocalypse depicts the phases of this combat, which, to our surprise, reproduces the main features of the epic struggle with Egypt. When the angels sound their trumpets (Apoc 8:2–9:21; 11:14–18) or pour out the vials of God's wrath (16:5–21), the plagues are unleashed, and like the Egyptians of old, the enemies of God's people are scourged with hail, fire, darkness, locusts, ulcers, bloody waters, frogs. . . . Such a chain of events can only lead up to a new exodus. John describes those who are delivered:

After this I saw a great multitude which no man could number, out of all nations and tribes and peoples and tongues, standing before the throne and before the Lamb, clothed in white robes, and with palms in their hands. And they cried with a loud voice, saying,

> "Salvation belongs to our God
> Who sits upon the throne,
>   and to the Lamb."

And all the angels were standing round about the throne, and the elders and the four living creatures; and they fell on their faces before the throne and worshipped God, saying,

> "Amen. Blessing and glory
>   and wisdom and thanksgiving
>   and honor and power and strength
>   to our God forever and ever. Amen."

And one of the elders spoke, and said to me, "These who are clothed in white robes, who are they? and whence have they come?" And I said to him, "My Lord, thou knowest." And he said to me, "These are they who have come out of the great tribulation, and have washed their robes and made them white in the blood of the Lamb. Therefore they are before the throne of God, and serve him day and night in his temple, and he who sits upon the throne will dwell with them. They shall neither hunger nor thirst any more, neither shall the sun strike them nor any heat. For the Lamb who is in the midst of the throne will shepherd them and will guide them to the fountains of the waters of life, and God will wipe away every tear from their eyes" (Apoc 7:9–17).

The blood of the lamb is not the only paschal theme in this section. The end of the vision repeats the very terms in which Isaiah (Chap 49) foretells the new Pasch and the new exodus. Again, when those "redeemed from the earth" sang a "new canticle" (Apoc 14:1–5) it was the canticle of Moses they sang, the canticle of triumph which was intoned after the crossing of the Red Sea by those who had been redeemed (Ex 15). To it they add the canticle of the lamb:

And I saw as it were a sea of glass mingled with fire, and those who had overcome the beast and its image and the number of its name, standing on the sea of glass, having the harps of God and singing the song of Moses, the servant of God, and the song of the Lamb, saying,

"Great and marvellous are thy works, O Lord God almighty;
   just and true are thy ways, O King of the ages.
Who will not fear thee, O Lord, and magnify thy name?
   for thou alone art holy.
For all nations will come and worship before thee;
   because thy judgements are manifest" (Apoc 15:2–4).

In the glory of the eternal Pasch, the first deliverance which foreshadowed it is not forgotten. The memory of the first paschal supper is still fresh:

And he said to me, "Write: Blessed are they who are called to the marriage supper of the Lamb" (Apoc 19:9).

The joy of the paschal banquet is re-echoed in the feast which Christ is willing to share even here below:

Behold, I stand at the door and knock. If any man listens to my voice and opens the door to me, I will come in to him and will sup with him, and he with me (Apoc 3:20).

Where else if not in the eucharist shall the Christian find the intimacy of supping with the Lord? This sacrament is the earthly Pasch, the foretaste of the Pasch of heaven, of which we shall partake when our exodus has ended, when "the sea is no more" (Apoc 21:1) to bar our entry to the promised land. There we shall live in the eternal city, in the light of the glorious lamb (*cf.* Apoc 22:3-5).

The meaning of the paschal mystery becomes clearer in its glorious consummation as described in the Apocalypse. The Scripture lessons of the breviary for the period after Easter have therefore been chosen from this, the last book of the Bible.

CHAPTER NINE

The Message of St. John's Gospel

St. John's gospel was, of course, never intended to be a complete biography of Christ. It is selective in what it records, and if John chooses some aspects and events of the life of Jesus for consideration, and omits others, it is perhaps because they were richer in meaning for him who had rested on the bosom of his Lord at the Last Supper. It is then not without reason that he makes the public life of our Lord gravitate around three Paschs.

At the first Pasch, Jesus makes known his mission by purifying the temple:

> The Jews therefore answered and said to him, "What sign dost thou show us, seeing that thou dost these things?" In answer Jesus said to them, "Destroy this temple and in three days I will raise it up." The Jews therefore said, "Forty-six years has this temple been in building, and wilt thou raise it up in three days?" But he was speaking of the temple of his body. When, accordingly, he had risen from the dead, his disciples remembered that he had said this, and they believed the Scripture and the word that Jesus had spoken (Jn 2:18–22).

From the very beginning of Christ's ministry, John sets in relief the sign of the resurrection. Under this first impulse, the fourth gospel moves dramatically towards the events of the last Pasch.

At the second Pasch, Jesus manifested his power by the miracle of the loaves. The story is also found in the synoptics, and Mark implies that it was springtime when he mentions that the people sat on the green grass (Mk 6:39). John is even more precise: "The passover, the feast of the Jews, was near" (Jn 6:4). This miracle, which was taken to be a messianic sign (Jn 6:15), was the cause of a serious crisis amongst the followers of Jesus:

> From this time many of his disciples turned back and no longer went about with him (Jn 6:67).

This change came about because the faith of many was too weak to accept the message of this miracle. By it Jesus wished to awaken in the hearts of his hearers the desire for another kind of food:

> "I am the bread of life. He who comes to me shall not hunger, and he who believes in me shall never thirst. . . .
> I am the living bread that has come down from heaven. If anyone eat of this bread he shall live forever; and the bread that I will give is my flesh for the life of the world."
> The Jews on that account argued with one another saying, "How can this man give us his flesh to eat?"
> Jesus therefore said to them, "Amen, amen I say to you, unless you eat the flesh of the Son of Man, and drink of his blood, you shall not have life in you. He who eats my flesh and drinks my blood has life everlasting and I will raise him up on the last day" (Jn 6:35, 51-55).

The repast of the new exodus will begin here below. Under the appearances of bread and wine, the flesh and blood of the sacrificial lamb will be life-giving food and drink.[1] At the mid-point of Christ's public life, John looks forward to the events which shall mark its end: the

---

1. *Cf.* Is 49:10 and also Christ's reference to the eucharist as manna, for another link with Exodus.

Last Supper, the cross, the resurrection, the three phases of the sacred mystery which brings men to eternal life.

The last Pasch of Jesus' public ministry is but the manifestation of his supreme love for his fellowmen:

> And before the feast of the passover, Jesus, knowing that the hour had come for him to pass out of this world to the Father, having loved his own who were in the world, loved them to the end (Jn 13:1).

The ancient Pasch was known as the "day" of Yahweh (*cf.* Ps 118(117):24). Jesus refers to his Pasch as his "hour" (Jn 17:1); it is for this hour that he came down on earth, an hour which shall know moments of darkness and light. He looked on the cross in terms of his final glory and his going forth from the cenacle—and from the world—found the following prayer on his lips:

> Father, the hour has come! Glorify thy Son, that thy Son may glorify thee. . . .
> But now I am coming to thee; and these things I speak in the world, in order that they may have my joy made full in themselves (Jn 17:1 and 17:13).

THE LAMB OF GOD

In the first pages of his gospel, John focuses our attention on yet another aspect of the paschal mystery of Jesus: the sacrifice of the lamb. He records the witness of John the baptist, with his insistence on the title "lamb of God":

> The next day John saw Jesus coming to him, and he said, "Behold, the lamb of God, who takes away the sin of the world!" (Jn 1:29).

> Again the next day John was standing there, and two of his disciples. And looking upon Jesus as he walked by, he said, "Behold, the lamb of God!" (Jn 1:35–36).

It is likely that John alludes to the suffering servant whose portrait is sketched for us by Isaiah:

> Though he was harshly treated, he submitted
>   and opened not his mouth;
> Like a lamb led to the slaughter
>   or a sheep before the shearers (Is 53:7).

> If he gives his life as an offering for sin,
>   he shall see his descendants in a long life,
>   and the will of Yahweh shall be accomplished through
>   him (Is 53:10).

> Therefore I will give him his portion among the great,
>   and he shall divide the spoils with the mighty,
> Because he surrendered himself to death
>   and was counted amongst the wicked;
> And *he shall take away the sins of many*,
>   and win pardon for their offences (Is 53:12).

To this image of the lamb of expiation, John adds the features of the paschal lamb, with which he portrays our crucified Saviour:

> The soldiers therefore came and broke the legs of the first, and of the other, who had been crucified with him. But when they came to Jesus, and saw that he was already dead, they did not break his legs; but one of the soldiers opened his side, with a lance, and immediately there came out blood and water.
>
> And he who saw it has borne witness, and his witness is true; and he knows that he tells the truth, that you also may believe. For these things came to pass that the Scripture might be fulfilled,
>   "Not a bone of him shall you break" (Jn 19:32–36).

Here there is no question of an oracle spoken by a prophet, but rather a single prescription of the ritual of the Jewish Pasch (Ex 12:46; Num 9:12) which prefigured the manner of offering the lamb of God. Not only the prophetic promises are fulfilled in the mystery of the son of God; all the religious realities of the Old Testament take on a new meaning in him. They were, as the epistle to the Hebrews has it, "the shadow of the good things to come" (Heb 10:1; cf. 8:5). God hid his secret design behind the realities of the Pasch and the exodus. It now stands forth in the strong light of fulfilment, and events which were limited in time have become eternally effective symbols of redemption.

While Christ was dying on the cross, lambs were being slain in the temple, perhaps by Jews who, that very morning, had called for the death of the lamb of God, and now felt righteous in their ritual purity:

> They therefore led Jesus from Caiaphas to the praetorium. Now it was early morning, and they themselves did not enter the praetorium, that they might not be defiled, but might eat the passover (Jn 18:28).

The Jews refused to enter the praetorium lest they be soiled by contact with a place frequented by pagans, and thus be prevented from partaking of the paschal lamb. This attitude of the Jewish leaders shows clearly that they had not eaten the Pasch, but intended to do so on the evening of Christ's death.

At that time, the ritual immolation of the paschal lambs used to commence in the afternoon:

> At what time did the sacrifice of the lamb take place? . . . The words of the Law, "between the two evenings," certainly pointed to the dusk, and the Sadducees held firmly to the opinion that the right time was between six and half-past seven in the evening. But we learn from Josephus that the Pharisees allowed the sacrifice to be

begun as early as half-past three, and if the pasch fell on a sabbath day, even an hour earlier.[2]

In the year of Christ's death, the Pasch apparently fell on the sabbath, and the day of the crucifixion was that of the *parasceve* or preparation for the sabbath (Mt 27:62; Mk 15:42; Lk 23:54; Jn 19:31 and 42). With the setting of the sun, the sabbath rest would begin.

At the ninth hour (3 P.M.) when Jesus expired on the cross, an enormous crowd was busily engaged in the temple. The Levites unceasingly poured the blood of the lambs on the altar, quite unaware that outside the city gates (Heb 13:12) the new paschal lamb was depriving their tasks of meaning, and giving to the world *peace*, light and life by *the blood of his cross* (Col 1:20).

2. M. J. Lagrange, O.P., *The Gospel of Jesus Christ*, Vol. II, p. 193 *f*.

The Paschal Feasts and the Paschal Vigil

The three synoptic gospels depict the Christian Pasch in terms of the eucharistic banquet of the Last Supper. John, on the other hand, finds it in the crucified Christ. It is only a question of emphasis, however, since the cross of Calvary alone gives meaning to the eucharistic sacrifice. The eucharist too contains the germ of future glory (*cf.* Jn 6:54). On Easter night, the Christ who is present on the altar is the lamb who is slain, yet lives with the Father. There he prepares a place for us, and while awaiting his return, we find in his passion a pledge of our future happiness:

> For as often as you shall eat this bread and drink the cup, you proclaim the death of the Lord, until he comes (1 Cor 11:26).

Every one of our Masses is therefore a Pasch, and every Sunday our weekly Pasch, but it is the ceremonies of holy week which bring to us each year the most impressive commemoration of the events which wrought our redemption. The Last Supper, the death and resurrection of Jesus are commemorated in succession, and the liturgy of holy week moves dramatically from scene to scene towards the glorious finale of the Easter vigil.

If we are to understand the meaning of these feasts, we must peruse the texts of the Old Testament which speak of the great vigil, and in doing so, follow the practice of the New Testament, which rarely fails to recall the ancient promises.

The liturgy too invites us to open our Bible. During the vigil ceremony, a triumphant song of thanksgiving is chanted by the deacon. In expressing her gratitude for the victory of Jesus and its newly-won liberty, the Church returns to those themes which are now familiar to us:

This is the night of our exodus, and of our victory in Christ, the feast of the true lamb, always living, whose blood protects us, and whose flesh becomes our food under the appearances of the new Azymes. Let us join with the Church in singing her hymn of paschal praise:

Just it is indeed and fitting
with all the ardor of our heart and mind
and with the service of our voice
to hymn God, the invisible almighty Father,
and his only-begotten Son, our Lord Jesus Christ,
who repaid Adam's debt for us to his eternal Father,
and with his dear blood
wiped out the penalty of that ancient sin.

This is the paschal feast
wherein is slain the true lamb
whose blood hallows the doorposts of the faithful.

This is the night
on which thou didst first cause our forefathers,
the sons of Israel,
in their passage out of Egypt,
to pass dry-shod over the Red Sea.

This is the night
which purged away the blackness of sin
by the light of the fiery pillar.

This is the night
which at this hour throughout the world
restores to grace and yokes to holiness
those who believe in Christ
detaching them from worldly vice
and all the murk of sin.

On this night
Christ
burst the bonds of death
and rose victorious from the grave.

Blessed indeed is this night,
the only night counted worthy
to know the season and the hour
in which Christ rose again from the grave.

Blessed indeed is this night
which despoiled the Egyptians
and enriched the Hebrews
the night
on which heaven is wedded to earth
the things of God to those of man.

The Exsultet[1]

1. The translation of the Exsultet is taken from the *Holy Week Manual* of Messrs. Burns & Oates.